Styles and Strategies
for **Teaching**
Middle School
MATHEMATICS

To my wife, Kathy, and my daughter, Kristine. Kathy and I each have a 30-year lead on our daughter in teaching mathematics. What is uncertain is when Kristine will gain ground; what is certain is that we will always work together as a family and a great team.

—Edward J. Thomas

To my wife, Sondra, whose lifelong loving support of my professional and personal interests has encouraged me beyond words—or numbers.

—John R. Brunsting

Styles and Strategies

for Teaching Middle School MATHEMATICS

21
TECHNIQUES FOR DIFFERENTIATING INSTRUCTION AND ASSESSMENT

Edward J. Thomas ▪ **John R. Brunsting**
Introduction by Harvey F. Silver

CORWIN
A SAGE Company

For information:

Corwin
A SAGE Company
2455 Teller Road
Thousand Oaks, California 91320
(800) 233-9936
Fax: (800) 417-2466
www.corwin.com

SAGE India Pvt. Ltd.
B 1/I 1 Mohan Cooperative
    Industrial Area
Mathura Road, New Delhi 110 044
India

SAGE Ltd.
1 Oliver's Yard
55 City Road
London EC1Y 1SP
United Kingdom

SAGE Asia-Pacific Pte. Ltd.
33 Pekin Street #02-01
Far East Square
Singapore 048763

Printed in the United States of America.

Library of Congress Cataloging-in-Publication Data

Thomas, Edward J. (Edward James), 1953-
Styles and strategies for teaching middle school mathematics: 21 techniques for differentiating instruction and assessment/Edward J. Thomas, John R. Brunsting.
    p. cm.
Includes bibliographical references and index.
ISBN 978-1-4129-6833-1 (pbk.)
    1. Mathematics—Study and teaching (Middle school) 2. Individualized instruction.
I. Brunsting, John R. II. Title.

QA135.6.T46 2010
510.71'2—dc22

2009051387

This book is printed on acid-free paper.

12   13   14   10   9   8   7   6   5   4   3   2

Acquisitions Editor:	Cathy Hernandez
Editorial Assistant:	Sarah Bartlett
Production Editor:	Libby Larson
Copy Editor:	Adam Dunham
Typesetter:	C&M Digitals (P) Ltd.
Proofreader:	Kevin Gleason
Indexer:	Judy Hunt
Cover Designer:	Karine Hovsepian

Contents

Acknowledgments

Much of this book is guided by the idea that all students can learn provided instruction is designed to reach every learner and all students are challenged to do their best work. The authors owe a great deal to two extraordinary educators who have been instrumental in our development as authors and teachers of mathematics—Harvey Silver and the late Richard Strong. Richard introduced us to learning styles, a strategic approach to teaching, and the art of addressing various learning styles in the classroom. Harvey taught us how to thoughtfully approach planning, assessment, and instruction, and how to refine instructional strategies to optimize student success. Together, Harvey and Richard embody the highest degrees of professionalism, passion, and productivity—and their work continues to provide teachers, instructional leaders, and administrators with a powerful model of instruction that engages and motivates students and teachers alike.

In a book of this length, there are many individuals whose work and diligence have kept us on track and on schedule. We would be lost without the editorial insight, wordsmithing, and meaningful conversations provided by Matthew Perini, the organizational and design skills of Justin Gilbert, and the collective efforts of the entire Thoughtful Education Press staff. We would also like to thank Cathy Hernandez and the entire team at Corwin for their patience and support throughout the development of this project.

PUBLISHER'S ACKNOWLEDGMENTS

Corwin gratefully acknowledges the contributions of the following reviewers:

Barry Farris
Dean, Department of Mathematics
    and Science
Columbia Academy
Columbia, TN

Kathryn McCormick
Mathematics Teacher
Gahanna Middle School
Westerville, OH

Rhonda Naylor
Mathematics Teacher
Campus Middle School
Englewood, CO

Cheryl Rose Tobey
Project Director
Education Development Center
Newton, MA

Andrew Rothstein
Curriculum Manager
National Academy Foundation
West Hartford, CT

Lois Williams
Middle School Mathematics
    Specialist
Scottsville, VA

About the Authors

Edward J. Thomas is founder and president of Dimension 2000, a professional development organization that works with teachers of mathematics. He has over 30 years of experience as a mathematics teacher at the middle school, high school, district, and undergraduate levels. Edward has authored several articles and books on mathematics instruction and has developed a number of educational games for the mathematics classroom. He was the cochair of the Northwest Georgia P–16 Council, an initiative designed to improve teacher quality and student achievement from preschool through the undergraduate level. Edward is an experienced mathematics consultant who has conducted workshops for schools throughout the country. He has also presented at state, regional, and national conferences for the National Council of Teachers of Mathematics (NCTM), Georgia Council of Teachers of Mathematics (GCTM), Southern Regional Education Board (SREB), Georgia Association of Educational Leaders (GAEL), Georgia Middle School Association (GMSA), and the Association for Supervision and Curriculum Development (ASCD).

John R. Brunsting is a mathematics teacher, a staff-development specialist, and an author. John serves schools as a teacher and coach as well as a mathematics consultant on practical, style-based tools and strategies. He is a coordinator for Illinois Advanced Placement Institutes and cofounder of Mathematics & Technology Institutes, teacher-training organizations committed to the instructional excellence of teachers. Previously an AP Calculus Exam Committee member, John coauthored *Preparing for the AP Calculus Examination* (2006). In 2008, John coauthored the bestselling *Math Tools, Grades 3–12: 64 Ways to Differentiate Instruction and Increase Student Engagement.* He has presented at national and international conferences for the National Council of Teachers of Mathematics (NCTM), National Council of Supervisors of Mathematics (NCSM), the Association for Supervision and Curriculum Development (ASCD), the Japan Association for Supervision and Curriculum Development (JASCD), Teachers Teaching with Technology (T^3), and the International Conference on Computers in Education (ICCE).

Introduction

Building the 21st-Century Mathematics Classroom

Imagine yourself as a second grader. In mathematics, you're adding, subtracting, multiplying, comparing fractions, and reading some basic graphs. Someone asks you, "Do you like math?" What would you say? Flash forward to fifth grade. The mathematics you're learning certainly has advanced, but so has your mind. How do you think you'd answer the question, "Do you like math?" Now, make one last jump. It's eighth grade, and you're making the transition from arithmetic to algebra. Once again, you're asked that simple question, "Do you like math?" What's your answer this time?

The fact is, studies show a disturbing trend in which "students in secondary school become increasingly less positive with regard to their attitude toward mathematics and their beliefs in the social importance of mathematics" (Wilkins & Ma, 2003, p. 58). For many students, this negative attitude becomes full-blown "math anxiety," an almost compulsive dislike of mathematics and mathematics instruction that emerges around fourth grade, reaches its peak in middle and high school (Scarpello, 2007), and sounds like this:

> I was terrified of math.
>
> I remember sitting in my seventh grade math class, staring at a quiz as if it were written in Chinese—it might as well have been a blank sheet of paper. Total brain freeze.
>
> Nothing made sense, I felt sick to my stomach, and I could feel the blood draining from my face. I had studied so hard, but it didn't seem to make any difference—I barely even recognized the math problems on the page.
>
> When the bell rang and my quiz was still blank, I wanted to disappear into my chair. I just didn't want to *exist*. (McKellar, 2008, p. xv)

These are the words of Danica McKellar, the actress who played Winnie Cooper on television's *The Wonder Years* and the author of *Math Doesn't Suck: How to Survive Middle School Math Without Losing Your Mind or Breaking a Nail.* While McKellar may be unique in that she became a famous actress before she was a teenager, her experiences as a middle school mathematics student are, sadly, all too common. For example, the classroom research that I have conducted with teachers and students over the last several years indicates that in third and fourth grade, almost 80% of students have positive attitudes towards mathematics and feel confident in their ability to succeed in mathematics. But as the mathematics curriculum becomes more difficult, more abstract, and more algebraic in middle school, the numbers change dramatically. By freshman year in high school, almost 50% of all students have developed an aversion to mathematics; they don't like it, they don't believe they're good at it, and many of them are proud to declare that they plan on taking the smallest number of mathematics courses in high school and beyond. This means that almost half of our students enter high school entertaining the dangerous idea that mathematics is a special realm for mathematicians and engineers, inscrutable to the average person and unnecessary for success in life.

This idea should give secondary teachers of mathematics the shivers. We know that mathematics is at the heart of so many things that affect everyone, from economics to technology, from the complexities of global marketing to the simple act of purchasing groceries. Mathematics, as Howard Gardner (1983, 1999, 2006) has shown us, is a vital form of human intelligence. Mathematics opens up career paths, empowers consumers, and makes all kinds of data meaningful—from basketball statistics to political polls to the latest trends in the stock market. Quite simply, we cannot afford to have so many secondary students who dread math class. We cannot allow half of our students to walk into a fast-moving, technological society looking to avoid confrontations with mathematics. For if we send an army of math-haters out into today's competitive global culture, we are short changing millions of students by severely limiting their chances of future success.

And yet, I have met many teachers of mathematics who are wondering openly if students really can be successful. "These kids hardly know basic mathematics. How can they be expected to do algebra?" is a common refrain from teachers in our middle schools. So what is the truth? Do we believe our students can be successful in mathematics or is the situation hopeless?

The good news is that research and experience both show that students' attitudes toward math and their problem-solving abilities are not fixed in place by the middle school years. In my 35 years of work in schools across the country, I have seen some truly remarkable changes in the way middle school students perceive mathematics and their ability to succeed in it. For example, I recently had the pleasure of working with a group of middle school mathematics teachers in Old Bridge, New Jersey. Together, we crafted a different kind of mathematics unit on three-dimensional figures. Instead of a test, we decided to build the unit around a summative assessment task (see Figure i.1 on page 3). This task required students to demonstrate just about everything they learned during the unit while also encouraging them to apply mathematics creatively. And in designing an instructional sequence to build the knowledge and skills students would need to succeed on the summative assessment task, we employed a variety of research-based strategies—strategies that we selected specifically

Final Task: A Monument to Learning

MathCorp has commissioned you to design and sketch a monument for a new math garden. The garden will have different sections, including sections devoted to important mathematicians and famous number sequences. The section of the garden they have asked you to design is the three-dimensional figure section.

Your task is to design and sketch a monument for the garden. The monument will be constructed of solid marble and must meet the following criteria:

1. In your design, you may only use the three-dimensional figures we learned about during our unit: *triangular prism, rectangular prism, triangular pyramid, rectangular pyramid, cylinder,* and *cone.*

2. You must include at least one of each of these three-dimensional figures in your design.

3. You must calculate the *volume* of your monument and show your work.

4. You must identify the total number of *bases, faces, edges,* and *vertices* within your monument.

5. You must include with your sketch a brief explanation of the thinking that went into your design. In your explanation, you must include at least ten critical vocabulary words from our investigation into three-dimensional figures and their volume.

FIGURE i.1 Summative Assessment Task

Source: Thoughtful Education Press. (2009). *Math Tools for Three-Dimensional Figures.* (Curriculum guide designed for the teachers of Old Bridge, New Jersey).

for their power to pique students' curiosity, actively engage students in learning, and speak to different styles of learners in the classroom.

When the teachers implemented their units in the classroom, the change in students' attitudes was palpable. Students were curious. They asked questions. They pursued difficult problems with vigor. Best of all, more students succeeded. In three of the four classrooms where the strategies were used, test scores rose by more than 3 full grade points. In one classroom, the average student score went from 73.71 to 81.41, an increase of over 10%—achieved with only one week of instruction. In the participating basic-skills classroom, test scores rose by 5.5 points, compared with an increase of only 1.5 points in the control group. By taking the time to engage students in the mathematics, the students were charged with learning; we also improved their comprehension, retention, and achievement levels.

This kind of change, of course, comes from teachers. And on this point, the research is sparklingly clear. A recent study tracking 3,000 seventh graders, for example, demonstrates that "teachers' choices of activities and mathematics problems can have a strong impact on the values that are portrayed in the classroom and on how students view mathematics and its usefulness" (Wilkins & Ma, 2003, p. 59). Of special note to middle school mathematics teachers is a meta-analytical study of 113 different studies suggesting that the middle school years are the most critical period for shaping students' attitudes towards mathematics and developing their confidence as mathematical problem solvers (Ma & Kishor, 1997).

So, how do middle school mathematics teachers use this critical time to engage and motivate more students to meet the new and higher demands of the 21st century, not to mention the challenges of expanding curriculums, state and national standards, school report cards, and greater expectations from colleges, government, and the public? The answer can be summed up in two simple but deep principles that drive this book and Ed Thomas's and John Brunsting's work in mathematics in general:

Effective mathematics instruction is *strategic*.

Effective mathematics instruction engages *all styles* of learners.

PRINCIPLE ONE: EFFECTIVE MATHEMATICS INSTRUCTION IS *STRATEGIC*

In what are two of the most comprehensive studies of the research behind various teaching strategies and their impact in the classroom, Robert Marzano (2007) and Robert Marzano, Debra Pickering, and Jane Pollock (2001) demonstrate conclusively that teaching strategies have a real and pervasive effect on student learning. Indeed, the evidence is clear: Classroom strategies like comparing and contrasting, developing and testing hypotheses, working cooperatively, creating visual representations, organizing information graphically, and using higher-order questions result in better performance and deeper learning among students. But as most teachers know, asking students to compare and contrast two time-distance-rate problems, for example, or to work cooperatively to solve a particularly rigorous problem may not result in the kinds of deep learning the research points to. It is in moments like these—when we apply research-based techniques only to experience a roomful of blank faces when what we were expecting was active engagement—that the gap between research and practice seems wider than ever. So, the question becomes, "How can I put this research into classroom practice so that it leads to a positive change in student learning?" To answer this question, let's look in on a classroom.

IN THE CLASSROOM, PART I

Situation: Alesandra Ciccio, a middle school mathematics teacher, has been teaching her students how to solve equations with one variable for the past week. Each day, Alesandra reviews the process, answers questions, provides in-class practice time, and assigns appropriate homework. She believes there is not much more she can do. Each day, when her students return to class, Alesandra finds they are still making many of the same mistakes. She is ready to test, move to the next unit, and admit that some of her students will never become proficient at the equation-solving process.

Applying a strategy: If Alesandra had a working knowledge of how and when to use teaching strategies for mathematics, she might have incorporated the Convergence Mastery strategy into her teaching. This strategy applied to Alesandra's situation would work as follows.

Once Alesandra realized that her students had reached an apparent plateau of proficiency, she would inform her students that they were going to participate in an engaging activity. She would prepare a series of five short quizzes on solving equations with one variable (see Figure i.2). Before each quiz, students would work cooperatively for 5 to 10 minutes to review and perfect the equation-solving process. Then, all students would be required to take the first quiz.

Quiz 1	Quiz 2	Quiz 3	Quiz 4	Quiz 5
1. $3x = 2x + 1$	1. $5x = 3x + 9$	1. $2z = z + 8$	1. $9a = 12a - 2$	1. $3c = 2c + 14$
2. $7b = 3b + 12$	2. $7c = 21 - 3c$	2. $6x = 4x - 2$	2. $5z = 24 - z$	2. $4a = 15 + a$
3. $4y = 8 - 2y$	3. $6y = 3 + 2y$	3. $4a = a + 6.5$	3. $3c = 2c + 9$	3. $9z = 11z - 18$
4. $5c = 2c + 9$	4. $11b = 5b + 6$	4. $y = 2y - 13$	4. $8b = 6b + 14$	4. $6x = 24 - 4x$
5. $6a = 4a + 10$	5. $3z = 4z - 5$	5. $5b = 3b + 7$	5. $2x = 4x - 9$	5. $y = 21 - 2y$

FIGURE i.2 Five Short Quizzes

At the end of the first quiz, students would cooperatively grade their solutions with Alesandra's help. Students who scored 100% would become permanent tutors and helpers and would exit the quiz-taking portion of the activity. Students who scored less than 100% would work cooperatively with the tutors and helpers to find their mistakes, correct them, and prepare for the next quiz. This process would continue until all five quizzes were taken. Since 100% success on a quiz is equivalent to an A in the grade book, students are highly motivated to communicate with each other, work cooperatively, and work hard to eliminate errors so they can take advantage of the immediate help and "retake" opportunities. As students progress through this process, they *converge toward mastery*.

What effect do you think Convergence Mastery would have in your classroom? Do you think students' mastery of the equation-solving process would improve as a result of the strategy?

Let's look in on another classroom where the students are having a different kind of problem.

IN THE CLASSROOM, PART II

Situation: Robert Gould is trying to curb his students' impulsivity as problem solvers. Too often, when Robert's students are faced with word problems, they will jump to solutions rather than engage in quality, presolution thinking and planning. This is especially worrisome to Robert since he knows that nearly one half of the items on his state's mathematics test are problems that students need to set up themselves.

Applying a strategy: Robert selects the strategy known as Math Notes because it is designed specifically to help students:

1. Identify the facts of the problem;
2. Determine exactly what the problem is asking;

(Continued)

(Continued)

3. Represent the problem visually; and

4. Plan out the steps that need to be taken to solve the problem.

He begins by presenting this problem to students:

"Bookworm Problem"

Volumes One and Two of a two-volume set of math books are next to one another on a shelf in their proper order (Volume One on the left, Volume Two on the right). Each front and back cover is $\frac{1}{4}$ inch thick and the pages portion of each book is 2 inches thick. If a bookworm starts at page 1 of Volume One and burrows all the way through to the last page of Volume Two, how far will the bookworm travel?

Next, he asks students to take a minute and try to solve the problem as they normally do. As Robert suspects, nearly all the students answer impulsively, coming up with either *5 inches* ($2\frac{1}{2}$ inches for each book times 2) or $4\frac{1}{2}$ *inches* ($2\frac{1}{2}$ inches for each book minus $\frac{1}{2}$ inch for the front and back cover). That's when Robert introduces and models Math Notes. Using the same problem, Robert shows students how he thinks through and sets up the problem on a Math Notes organizer (Figure i.3).

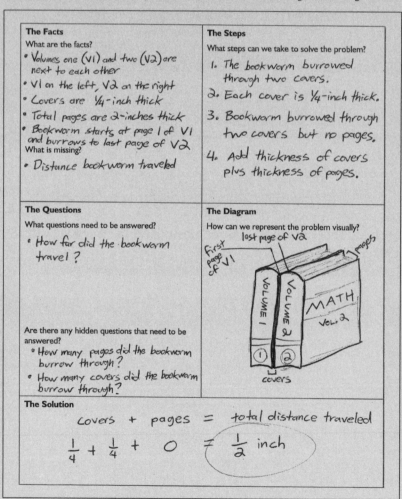

The Facts
What are the facts?
- Volumes one (V1) and two (V2) are next to each other
- V1 on the left, V2 on the right
- Covers are ¼-inch thick
- Total pages are 2-inches thick
- Bookworm starts at page 1 of V1 and burrows to last page of V2
What is missing?
- Distance bookworm traveled

The Steps
What steps can we take to solve the problem?
1. The bookworm burrowed through two covers.
2. Each cover is ¼-inch thick.
3. Bookworm burrowed through two covers but no pages.
4. Add thickness of covers plus thickness of pages.

The Questions
What questions need to be answered?
- How far did the bookworm travel?

Are there any hidden questions that need to be answered?
- How many pages did the bookworm burrow through?
- How many covers did the bookworm burrow through?

The Diagram
How can we represent the problem visually?

The Solution
covers + pages = total distance traveled
$$\frac{1}{4} + \frac{1}{4} + 0 = \frac{1}{2} \text{ inch}$$

FIGURE i.3 Completed Math Notes Organizer

What students see very clearly as a result of Robert's use of Math Notes is that without a strategy for breaking down, attacking, and visualizing difficult word problems, they are likely to miss essential information or misinterpret what the problem is asking them to do.

Over the course of the year, students keep a notebook of problems they've solved using Math Notes. This way, they can refer back to their notebooks and look for models they can use whenever they come across new problems.

Convergence Mastery and Math Notes are only two of the 21 research-based teaching strategies that Ed Thomas and John Brunsting lay out in this book. Convergence Mastery is, as its name suggests, a Mastery strategy—a strategy focused on helping students remember mathematical procedures and practice their computational skills. But mathematics, of course, is about more than memory and practice. It is also about asking questions, making and testing hypotheses, thinking flexibly, visualizing concepts, working collaboratively, and exploring real-world applications. To accommodate this cognitive diversity, the strategies in this book are broken up into five distinct categories. Four of these categories—Mastery, Understanding, Self-Expressive, and Interpersonal—develop specific mathematical skills. The fifth category, Multistyle strategies, contains strategies like Math Notes, strategies that foster several kinds of mathematical thinking simultaneously. The following map (Figure i.4) explains these five categories.

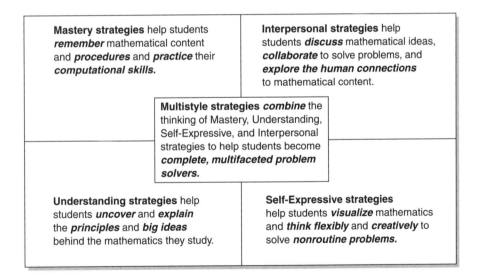

Mastery strategies help students *remember* mathematical content and *procedures* and *practice* their *computational skills.*

Interpersonal strategies help students *discuss* mathematical ideas, *collaborate* to solve problems, and *explore the human connections* to mathematical content.

Multistyle strategies *combine* the thinking of Mastery, Understanding, Self-Expressive, and Interpersonal strategies to help students become *complete, multifaceted problem solvers.*

Understanding strategies help students *uncover* and *explain* the *principles* and *big ideas* behind the mathematics they study.

Self-Expressive strategies help students *visualize* mathematics and *think flexibly* and *creatively* to solve *nonroutine problems.*

FIGURE i.4 Map of Mathematical Strategies

Each of the strategies in these five categories represents a different kind of thinking, a different way of interacting with mathematical content, a different opportunity to grow as a learner and problem solver. Take just one of these ways of thinking away, and you really don't know mathematics. Think about it: If you can't compute accurately (Mastery), explain mathematical concepts (Understanding), find ways to solve non-routine problems (Self-Expressive), or explore and discuss real-world applications with fellow problem solvers (Interpersonal), then you don't have the complete picture; and without a complete picture, you don't *really* know mathematics. This simple but often-overlooked idea—that mathematical learning and problem solving require the cultivation of different kinds of thinking—brings us to the second way that this book will help you and your students achieve higher levels of success: *learning styles*.

PRINCIPLE TWO: EFFECTIVE MATHEMATICS INSTRUCTION ENGAGES *ALL STYLES* OF LEARNERS

Let's listen in on two secondary students who were asked the same question:

"Who was your favorite mathematics teacher and why?"

Alisha: My favorite math teacher so far has definitely been Ms. Tempiano. She really taught, and by that I mean she was very clear about explaining what we were learning and always showed us exactly how to do it. Whenever we learned a new skill or a new technique, not only would she review the steps, she would work with us to develop a way to help us remember how to apply the steps, like the acronym "Please Excuse My Dear Aunt Sally" for remembering the order of operations. Once we knew the steps, she would let us practice the steps to different problems. Sometimes we practiced alone and sometimes we practiced in groups, but Ms. Tempiano always walked around the room and worked with us like a coach. I loved getting feedback right away. That really helped me when she would walk around and watch what we were doing and help us with any problems we were having.

Ethan: I didn't really think I liked or was good at math before I had Mr. Hollis for Algebra I. He did this thing called "Problem Solving Fridays." Every Friday, we focused on what he called "nonroutine" problems, which were basically these really cool problems about things like building bridges or developing a new lottery game, problems that didn't have simple answers. So, we had to experiment, try different things out—you know, get creative—to see how we might be able to find a solution. Actually, I knew I would like Mr. Hollis on the first day of class.

I was a freshman and math was first period. I walked in expecting the same old thing: worksheets, the odd problems, quizzes. But instead, Mr. Hollis spent the first day on metaphors! He challenged us to create a metaphor for the problem-solving process. I showed how each step in the problem-solving process was like one of the stages in human digestion. It was really cool—I showed how you "chew" and "breakdown" and "process" both equations and food. The class loved it. And you know what else? I never forgot the steps in solving equations after that.

Almost immediately, we can see that Alisha and Ethan treat mathematics very differently. Alisha is attracted to problems that have clear solutions.

Ethan, on the other hand, gets excited about nonroutine problems where finding a solution requires experimentation and flexibility.

Alisha solves problems by selecting an algorithm and applying it step by step, while Ethan's problem-solving process is one of generating and exploring alternatives. As far as teachers of mathematics go, Alisha prefers one who is clear about expectations, models new skills, allows students to practice the skills, and provides regular feedback and coaching along the way. From Ethan's point of view, an ideal mathematics teacher allows students to explore the content through the imagination and creative problem solving. Finally, and most significantly, each student sees different purposes for learning and using mathematics. For Alisha, mathematics represents structure and stability, a set of failsafe procedures that can be used again and again to find correct solutions. Ethan, of course, would disagree. For him, mathematics is a medium for expressing powerful ideas and creating new and interesting products—a kind of intellectual playground full of possibilities, unseen connections, and fascinating applications. The differences in how these two students experience and approach mathematics are the result of *learning styles.*

Learning styles come from psychologist Carl Jung's (1923) seminal work on the human mind. Jung, one of the founding fathers of modern psychology, discovered that the way we take in information and then judge the importance of that information develops into different personality types. Working from Jung's foundational work on personality types, Kathleen Briggs and Isabel Myers (1962/1998) later expanded Jung's model to create a comprehensive model of human difference, which they made famous with their Myers-Briggs Type Indicator (1962/1998).

Since the development of the Myers-Briggs Type Indicator, new generations of researchers have worked to apply and adopt the personality-types model to the specific demands of teaching and learning. Bernice McCarthy (1982), Carolyn Mamchur (1996), Edward Pajak (2003), Gayle Gregory (2005), and Harvey Silver, Richard Strong, and Matthew Perini (2007) are some of the key researchers who have helped educators convert and expand the insights of Jung and Myers and Briggs into a more practical and classroom-friendly model of cognitive diversity—learning styles.

A few years back, I initiated a new research study with one of the authors of this book, Ed Thomas. Our goal was to make a deep connection between mathematics and learning styles. We reviewed the research on learning styles, worked with teachers of mathematics and their students in classrooms, and developed a new instrument for assessing students' mathematical learning styles—*The Math Learning Style Inventory for Secondary Students* (Silver, Thomas, & Perini, 2003). Out of our work, we identified four distinct styles of mathematical learners, which are outlined in Figure i.5 on page 10.

It is important to remember that no student—no person—is a perfect representative of a single style. Learning styles are not pigeonholes; it is neither possible nor productive to reduce this student to a Self-Expressive

Mastery Math Students	Interpersonal Math Students
Want to learn practical information and set procedures.	**Want to** learn math through dialogue, collaboration, and cooperative learning.
Like math problems that are like problems they have solved before and that use algorithms to produce a single solution.	**Like math problems that** focus on real-world applications and on how mathematics helps people.
Approach problem solving in a step-by-step manner.	**Approach problem solving** as an open discussion among a community of problem solvers.
Experience difficulty when mathematics becomes too abstract or when faced with nonroutine problems.	**Experience difficulty when** instruction focuses on independent seatwork or when what they are learning seems to lack real-world application.
Want a math teacher who models new skills, allows time for practice, and builds in feedback and coaching sessions.	**Want a math teacher who** pays attention to their successes and struggles in mathematics.
Understanding Math Students	**Self-Expressive Math Students**
Want to understand why the math they learn works.	**Want to** use their imagination to explore mathematical ideas.
Like math problems that ask them to explain, prove, or take a position.	**Like math problems that** are nonroutine, project-like in nature, and that allow them to think outside the box.
Approach problem solving by looking for patterns and identifying hidden questions.	**Approach problem solving** by visualizing the problem, generating possible solutions, and exploring among the alternatives.
Experience difficulty when there is a focus on the social environment of the classroom (e.g., on collaboration and cooperative problem solving).	**Experience difficulty when** mathematics instruction is focused on drill and practice and rote problem solving.
Want a math teacher who challenges them to think and who lets them explain their thinking.	**Want a math teacher who** invites imagination and creative problem solving into the mathematics classroom.

FIGURE i.5 Four Styles of Mathematics Students

Source: Silver, H. F., Thomas, E., & Perini, M. J. (2003). *Math Learning Style Inventory for Secondary Students.* (p. 8).

learner or that student to an understanding learner. Various contexts and types of problems call for different kinds of thinking, and all students rely on all four styles to help them learn mathematics. However, it is equally true that people tend to have style preferences; like all people, each student will usually show strength in one or two styles and weakness in one or two others. What all this means is that learning styles are the key to motivating students, improving their attitudes toward mathematics, and helping them experience higher levels of success. Tapping into the power of learning styles is a matter of building on students' strengths by accommodating their preferred styles while simultaneously encouraging them to stretch their talents and grow as learners by developing less-preferred styles.

Recent research conducted by Robert Sternberg (2006) shows that rotating teaching strategies to reach all styles of learners is about more than being fair; it's about being effective. Sternberg and his colleagues conducted a remarkable series of studies involving diverse student populations from around the world. As part of these studies, students were taught mathematical content in five different ways. Some students were taught using

1. A memory-based approach emphasizing factual recall;

2. An analytical approach emphasizing critical thinking;

3. A creative approach emphasizing imagination;

4. A practical approach emphasizing real-world applications; and

5. A diverse approach incorporating all four approaches.

Which group of students who participated in these studies do you think did best? Hands down it was the students who were taught using all four approaches. They did better on objective tests, and they did better on performance assessments. From these studies, Sternberg (2006) concludes, "even if our goal is just to maximize students' retention of information, teaching for diverse styles of learning still produces superior results. This approach apparently enables students to capitalize on their strengths and to correct or to compensate for their weaknesses, encoding material in a variety of interesting ways" (pp. 33–34).

So, how do we accomplish this goal of teaching for diverse styles? Take another look at our map of strategies below (Figure i.6).

What the map shows us is how styles and strategies come together, the place where they meet. Accommodating students' strong styles and

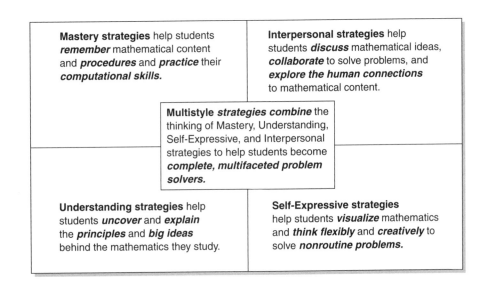

FIGURE i.6   Map of Mathematical Strategies

fostering their weaker styles requires us to vary the strategies we select and use in our classrooms. When you use a Self-Expressive strategy, for example, not only are you inviting your creative students who think mathematics is too black and white into the learning process, you are also challenging all of your "procedure whizzes" to step back and think about mathematics in a new and illuminating way. The same is true for the Mastery, Understanding, and Interpersonal strategies: The different kinds of thinking required by each style of strategy will engage some students and challenge others, while the Multistyle strategies combine the thinking of all four styles inside a single strategy.

The key to making all of this work in the classroom is *rotation*. Use all five types of strategies regularly. Keep track of what styles you use and when. Here's an experiment: If a concept seems to be eluding students, try using a strategy like Metaphorical Expression (Self-Expressive) or Compare and Contrast (Understanding). If students of all styles need to work on complex problem solving, try a Multistyle strategy like Math Notes.

Remember that good problem solving requires all four styles of thinking; therefore, teaching students how to become good problem solvers will require you to rotate around the "wheel of style."

THE 21ST-CENTURY CLASSROOM: WITHIN OUR REACH

What Ed Thomas and John Brunsting have found, through decades of teaching mathematics and conducting professional development seminars for teachers of mathematics, is that building a 21st-century mathematics classroom means "making students as important as standards." But rhetoric is one thing; a mathematics classroom that is humming with the thought of actively engaged students is quite another.

What Ed and John show is that getting the classroom we all wish for is not pie-in-the-sky idealism. Thankfully, building a 21st-century mathematics classroom does not require us to reinvent ourselves or our beliefs. By developing a working knowledge of the research-based strategies in this book and by rotating them so that you accommodate and grow the learning styles of all your students, you can increase significantly the power of your teaching and your students' learning.

We know this book will be an important tool in developing such a classroom.

Harvey

Tr. Harvey F. Silver, EdD

1

Mastery Strategies

OVERVIEW

Mastery strategies help students *remember* mathematical content and *procedures* and *practice* their *computational skills*. They are especially engaging to Mastery math students.

Mastery math students . . .

- *Want to* learn practical information and set procedures.
- *Like math problems that* are like problems they have solved before and that use algorithms to produce a single solution.
- *Approach problem solving* in a step-by-step manner.
- *Experience difficulty when* mathematics becomes too abstract or when faced with nonroutine problems.
- *Want a math teacher who* models new skills, allows time for practice, and builds in feedback and coaching sessions.

The six Mastery strategies in this chapter can help you meet these NCTM Process Standards (see Figure 1.0).

Strategy	NCTM Process Standards*				
	Problem Solving	Reasoning and Proof	Communication	Connections	Representation
Convergence Mastery [p. 15] – Students prepare individually and take quizzes with peer review until all students demonstrate complete mastery of the content.			✓		
Vocabulary Knowledge Rating [p. 18] – At different points throughout a unit, students rate their knowledge of critical vocabulary terms.			✓		
Proceduralizing [p. 24] – Students internalize a procedure by observing their teacher demonstrating it, writing its steps in their own words, and using it to solve problems cooperatively and individually.	✓		✓		
Mental Math Strings [p. 30] – For a few minutes each day in class, students are challenged to perform mathematical operations and solve problems mentally.		✓		✓	
Graduated Difficulty [p. 36] – Students assess their level of competence by successfully completing a task from an array of options at different levels of difficulty.	✓	✓			
New American Lecture [p. 42] – Students are "hooked" into a presentation and use a visual organizer and deep-processing questions to make notes, organize information, and remember essential content.			✓	✓	

FIGURE 1.0 Correlation of Mastery Strategies to NCTM Process Standards

*For more information on the National Council of Teachers of Mathematics (NCTM) Process Standards, please consult their *Principles and Standards for School Mathematics* (2000), or visit their website at www.nctm.org.

Convergence Mastery

Strategy Overview

In every math classroom, after every quiz or test, a wonderful instructional opportunity presents itself: the opportunity to help students learn from their mistakes. But the truth is, in most math classrooms, tests are returned with red marks on them, and the next unit begins. This means that the great majority of math students are missing the chance to root out errors, clarify confusions, and grow as learners.

The Convergence Mastery strategy is a simple but powerful way to provide students with multiple opportunities to learn from their mistakes and achieve mastery of important math procedures and skills. At the heart of the strategy is a series of short quizzes focused on a single core skill (e.g., factoring polynomials). Before taking the first quiz, students practice the skill and review in pairs or small groups. Students take the first quiz individually, return to their groups, and grade one another's quizzes as the teacher provides the correct answers. Only two grades are possible:

1. Students with one or more incorrect answers receive an *Incomplete*

2. Students who answer every question correctly receive an *A*

Students who receive an A are not required to take additional quizzes. Instead, they help group members who received an incomplete to review, make corrections, and prepare for the next quiz. The strategy continues until all students have received an A.

How to Use the Strategy

1. Select a math procedure or skill you want all students to master.

2. Develop three to five short quizzes that contain problems representative of the skill.

3. Explain the quiz process and grading procedures to students. Be sure they understand how the process is designed to help them.

4. Provide a few minutes for students to review the skill in small groups.

5. Administer a quiz to all students. Quizzes are timed (usually 5 minutes per quiz).

6. Share the correct answers, and have students grade other group members' quizzes.

7. Excuse any students who received an A from further quizzes. Have these students help their group members correct errors and prepare for the next quiz. If necessary, provide coaching sessions to struggling students.

8. Continue the process (Steps 5–7) until virtually all students have received an A.

The Strategy in Action: Examples

Figure 1.1 shows sample topics ideal for the Convergence Mastery strategy.

Numbers	Algebra	Geometry	Measurement	Probability	Statistics
Operations on whole numbers	Evaluating expressions	Analysis of plane figures	Calculating perimeter	Finding P(A)	Computing mean, median, and mode
Operations on fractions	Solving equations	Computing numbers of diagonals	Calculating area	Finding P(A or B)	Interpreting histograms
Operations on integers	Factoring expressions	Transforming figures	Calculating surface area	Finding P(A and B)	Creating box-and-whisker plots
Prime factorization	Working with irrational numbers	Drawing nets of 3D figures	Converting metric units	Permutations and combinations	Interpreting graphs

FIGURE 1.1 Ideal Convergence Mastery Topics

Figure 1.2 shows a sample set of quizzes for solving equations.

Quiz 1	Quiz 2	Quiz 3	Quiz 4	Quiz 5
Solve each equation and show your work.	Solve each equation and show your work.	Solve each equation and show your work.	Solve each equation and show your work.	Solve each equation and show your work.
1. $2(4x + 5) = 26$	1. $2(6x + 4) = 32$	1. $5(2x + 5) = 35$	1. $4(2x + 3) = 36$	1. $6(x + 2) = 48$
2. $.5(6x - 8) = 15$	2. $.5(8x - 3) = 7$	2. $.5(4x - 8) = 10$	2. $.5(3x - 1) = 11$	2. $.5(10x - 8) = 11$
3. $-3(3x + 2) = -24$	3. $-4(x + 5) = -60$	3. $-2(3x + 7) = -4$	3. $-3(2x + 1) = -27$	3. $-2(4x + 8) = -10$

FIGURE 1.2 Sample Convergence Mastery Quizzes—Solving Equations

Why the Strategy Works

Sometimes, teaching strategies come from real-life experiences. The initial seed for the Convergence Mastery strategy was planted at Boy Scouts camp where one of the authors of this book (Ed Thomas) spent his summers as a young boy. At summer camp, scouts had opportunities to earn awards and merit badges for meeting various challenges. One challenge was to make fire without matches. On certain nights, scouts were given a rock, a piece of steel, and 30 minutes to produce a fire. Scouts who succeeded were given a "Singed Eyebrows" certificate. Scouts who failed were invited to try again the next time the Singed Eyebrows station was open. Whenever a scout produced fire, whether it was on the first try or the fourth, he received his Singed Eyebrows certificate. This open-door policy on success motivated scouts to keep trying, learn from their mistakes, and achieve mastery in the skill of making fire.

Convergence Mastery takes the wisdom of Boy Scouts camp and puts it to work in the mathematics classroom. The strategy provides students with repeated and controlled practice opportunities, which help build students' debugging skills and maximize skill acquisition. Convergence Mastery also provides teachers with an easy way to differentiate instruction according to students' readiness levels. Students who need more practice opportunities and more coaching receive both. At the same time, students who have already mastered the skill do not sit around idly; instead, they become part of the teaching and learning process. What's more, by having students help other students who have yet to receive an A on a quiz, Convergence Mastery capitalizes on the power of peer-coaching partnerships, which have been shown to increase students' academic intensity (Fuchs, Fuchs, Mathes, & Simmons, 1997) and lead to academic gains and more positive attitudes toward subject matter (King-Sears & Bradley, 1995).

Planning Considerations

The idea behind Convergence Mastery is that all students *converge towards mastery* of the highlighted skill or procedure by achieving a perfect score on a short quiz. In terms of preparing for Convergence Mastery in the classroom, most of the planning time goes to the development of the quizzes. Here are a few guidelines to keep in mind when developing Convergence Mastery quizzes:

Select a focus skill that students are familiar with and have partially mastered. For example, if students have experience with solving linear equations but have been making mistakes in the process, then solving linear equations would be an ideal candidate for Convergence Mastery.

Make the quizzes brief. Remember, during a single class period, students will be taking up to five quizzes while also spending 5 minutes of study time between each quiz. Make sure that each quiz can be completed by students in 5 minutes.

Keep the focus skill and the level of difficulty constant across all the quizzes. Only the problems should vary from quiz to quiz.

Consider projecting the quizzes. To save paper and time, you might consider writing the quizzes on a transparency or designing them in a program like Microsoft PowerPoint and then projecting them through a multimedia device.

Variations and Extensions

Depending on the difficulty of the focus skill and students' level of proficiency, you may choose to play a more active teaching and coaching role between quizzes. If you choose to run the between-quiz coaching sessions yourself, you may want to vary the role of students who earn the A grade and exit the quiz-taking activity. For example, you might allow them to begin their homework, or ask them to design and solve problems at a higher level of difficulty than those on the quizzes. These students can also be invited to participate in subsequent quizzes and earn extra credit points, which increases the sense of reward for having mastered the skill early.

Vocabulary Knowledge Rating (VKR)

Strategy Overview

Successful students know how to assess and evaluate their own learning. They tend to have a clear understanding of what they know and which concepts and ideas they still need to learn. Vocabulary Knowledge Rating (VKR) gives teachers of mathematics a strategic approach to vocabulary instruction—an approach that helps students evaluate the state of their learning and build a deep understanding of critical content.

VKR provides teachers with a wealth of formative assessment data by providing answers to two questions: One, which concepts are giving the entire class difficulty? And two, which individual students are struggling most with the content of the unit?

In VKR, students numerically rate their understanding of key terms using an organizer like the one shown in Figure 1.3.

Fractions				
Vocabulary Term	**I've never heard of the term**	**I've seen or heard of the term before**	**I think I know the term**	**I know the term and can explain it**
common denominator	1	2	(3)	4
denominator	1	2	(3)	4
equivalent fractions	1	(2)	3	4
fraction	1	2	3	(4)
improper fraction	1	(2)	3	4
inverting	(1)	2	3	4
least common denominator	1	(2)	3	4
mixed numbers	1	2	(3)	4
numerator	1	2	(3)	4
proper fraction	1	(2)	3	4
My Vocabulary Knowledge Rating:	(25)		**Today's Date:** Oct 8, 2009	

FIGURE 1.3 Student's VKR for a Unit on Fractions

Because self-assessment is always an ongoing process, VKR is most effective when it is used regularly. Typically, students complete a VKR organizer at least three times over the course of a mathematics unit:

- *Before the unit begins* to assess their initial understanding and help them activate any relevant background knowledge.
- *During the unit* to assess what they currently know and understand and to determine which words and concepts require more study.
- *After the unit is completed,* but prior to the test or culminating assessment, to focus study efforts and to reflect on the learning process.

How to Use the Strategy

1. Prioritize your vocabulary by selecting the 10 to 12 most important words from your unit that students should focus on. Limit your selections to only the most critical words that every student will need to know and understand.

2. Distribute a VKR organizer to each student (see Organizer A on page 23 for a blank reproducible). Review the ranking system with students:

   1 = I have never heard of this term.

   2 = I have seen or heard of this term, but I am not sure what it means.

   3 = I think I know what this term means.

   4 = I know this term, and can explain what it means.

3. Have students rate their current knowledge of each vocabulary word by selecting the appropriate number on the four-point scale. To complete the organizer, students record the sum of their points in the Knowledge Rating box and date their work.

4. Have students revisit their initial VKR organizers throughout the unit to reassess their knowledge and monitor how their understanding of key content has expanded and still needs to grow.

5. Help students prepare for an end-of-unit test or culminating assessment by giving them time to review and reflect on their previously completed VKR organizers and to discuss their learning with classmates.

Implementation Note: Formative assessment data from students' VKR organizers can also be used to provide parents and educational support service specialists with valuable information to help focus conversations with each student about his or her learning.

The Strategy in Action: Examples

Here are some sample middle school mathematics units with corresponding vocabulary terms:

Measurement: area, altitude, base, circumference, diameter, grid, length, unit of measurement, perimeter, radius, volume

Geometry: circle, hexagon, octagon, parallelogram, pentagon, polygon, quadrilateral, rectangle, rhombus, square, trapezoid, triangle

Statistics: box and whisker plot, data, mean, measures of central tendency, median, mode, range, quartile, rank, stem and leaf plot, tally, variance

Why the Strategy Works

In their research into vocabulary instruction, Jenkins, Stein, and Wysocki (1984) show that students need to be exposed to new words at least six times to master and retain their meanings. VKR provides teachers with a manageable way to keep students closely connected to the key terms and concepts in a unit, giving them the exposure they need to learn new words deeply.

Another important aspect of vocabulary instruction is focusing on only the most important concepts and terms. In fact, Marzano (2004) shows that when vocabulary instruction is focused on critical academic terms (as opposed to high-frequency word lists), student achievement can increase by as much as 33 percentile points on content-area tests. This is why VKR concentrates both the teacher's and students' attention on only 10 to 12 terms.

A final benefit of VKR is that it builds the habits and skills of self-regulated learning, which has been identified as a hallmark of intelligent behavior (Costa & Kallick, 2000).

Planning Considerations

While VKR is not a difficult strategy to implement, there are a few important guidelines to consider:

Select only the most critical words. Resist the temptation to list every word that students might encounter during the unit, and include only the 10 to 12 critical words that will be most helpful to students. In some cases, you may choose to include words that are not quite central to the unit but will help scaffold student learning. For example, in selecting words for a unit on fractions, a teacher chose to include the term *number line* because she wanted students to compare and order fractions using a number line.

Determine when and how you will help students assess their learning. Identify the segments of your unit in which you will present and discuss a number of the words and concepts from your list. In between these segments, give students ample opportunity to self-assess their knowledge and reflect on their progress. Make sure that all students know that these are valuable periods of class time that should be used for meaningful reflection and discussion.

Decide when it will be appropriate to analyze students' progress. Ask yourself, At what points would it be helpful for me to know whether students have learned the key words and concepts? After a weekend? Before a school break? At the completion of smaller sections within the unit?

Variations and Extensions

Create Your Own VKR

After you and your students have used a traditional VKR organizer, consider inviting your class to revise or improve upon the form by creating a new set of descriptive column headings. For example, after a group discussion, a class of sixth graders developed a three-point VKR scale with the following headings:

1 = I really don't know this word.

2 = I have seen or heard this word.

3 = I really know this word because I can give an example.

You can also extend the strategy by inviting students to develop their own creative, personally meaningful VKR organizers. For example, Figure 1.4 shows how an eighth grader incorporated her love of softball into her VKR organizer.

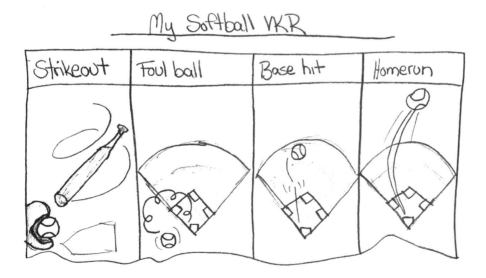

FIGURE 1.4 Student's VKR Using Softball Icons

Definition Doctor

Definition Doctor (adapted from Thomas, 2008) is a great way to review VKR words and to formatively assess students' vocabulary knowledge using an engaging whole-class game format. It works especially well in conjunction with VKR because VKR automatically aligns the activity with a set number of critical terms that have already been the focus of instruction. You can use Definition Doctor at various points within the VKR cycle by following these simple steps:

1. Have all students take out their VKR organizers.

2. Begin by playing the role of the Definition Doctor yourself. Select a student (Student A) to choose one word for you—the Definition Doctor—to define and explain why the word is important to the lesson or unit.

3. After you define and explain the word, Student A assumes the role of the Definition Doctor and a new student (Student B) chooses a word for the good doctor to define and explain. (If the Definition Doctor is having trouble, you may choose to allow him or her to get a "second opinion" by allowing for a "consult" with you or another student.)

4. Student B now becomes the Definition Doctor and a new student selects a word.

5. Continue this process until all the words from the list have been defined and explained.

6. Keep track of any words that seemed to give students difficulty and review them with the class.

Organizer A: Vocabulary Knowledge Rating Organizer

Topic:				
Vocabulary Term	**I've never heard of the term**	**I've seen or heard of this term before**	**I think I know this term**	**I know the term and can explain it**
	1	2	3	4
	1	2	3	4
	1	2	3	4
	1	2	3	4
	1	2	3	4
	1	2	3	4
	1	2	3	4
	1	2	3	4
	1	2	3	4
	1	2	3	4
	1	2	3	4
	1	2	3	4
My Vocabulary Knowledge Rating:			**Today's Date:**	

Proceduralizing

Strategy Overview

Mathematics is brimming with procedures: long division, finding the greatest common factor, completing the square, differentiating the product of two functions, just to name a few. Often, the difference between successfully and unsuccessfully internalizing mathematical procedures proves the difference between high and low achievers in mathematics. In classrooms throughout the country, teachers of mathematics spend significant classroom time demonstrating procedures while students watch, copy their teacher's work, and strive to keep pace before trying a few practice problems on their own.

But jump ahead a few weeks and many students won't be able to recall the steps well enough to apply the procedure (or skill) and successfully solve a problem. In order for students to master, internalize, and retain the steps of important mathematical procedures, students need to do more than watch, copy, and keep pace with their teacher's work; students need to make mathematical procedures their own.

The Proceduralizing strategy helps students make even the most challenging mathematical procedures their own through observation, mathematical analysis, collaboration, and independent practice. Students observe a teacher solving different sample problems using the procedure; analyze the procedure by identifying its general steps and writing the steps in their own words; collaborate with a partner to solve two problems, once by coaching and once by calculating; and independently practice and refine their knowledge by applying the procedure to solve a set of problems.

How to Use the Strategy

1. Select a mathematical procedure that is important for your students to learn. The procedure should be accessible to students and be relevant to current (or future) classroom applications.

2. Model the procedure with students using sample problems. The sample problems should not be overly complex; rather, they should clearly illustrate the general steps in the procedure.

3. Review the sample problems with students, and focus on the essential steps in the procedure. Don't overwhelm students with additional information like prerequisite procedures or secondary processes.

4. Work with students to identify a set of generalized steps for the procedure. Have students write these steps in their own words. Encourage students to ask questions about the procedure and steps to help them internalize the information.

5. Organize students into pairs. Have students review the procedure together to make sure that they've internalized all of the steps.

6. Provide each pair of students with two problems. One student works on solving the first problem (without seeing the steps) while the other student coaches using the steps. For the second problem, students switch roles. While students are working collaboratively, circulate around the room to monitor students' progress and answer any questions.

7. Encourage students to share their experiences with the entire class, including both successes and difficulties they had solving the problems collaboratively.

8. Assign additional problems for students to solve independently using the same procedure. This work can be completed in class or for homework.

The Strategy in Action

Jackie Parra teaches sixth-grade mathematics and has identified graphing equations of the form $y = mx + b$ as an important procedure for all of her students to know well. To help her students master this essential graphing procedure, Jackie uses the Proceduralizing strategy.

Jackie starts by graphing a few linear equations using the slope-intercept form, $y = mx + b$, and summarizes the procedure into five general steps that her students can easily understand:

1. Write the equation in the form $y = mx + b$.

2. Use graphing paper to plot the number b on the y-axis. (This point is the y-intercept of the graph.)

3. Write the slope m as a fraction $\frac{k}{h}$.

4. From the y-intercept, move h units horizontally and k units vertically on the plane. Plot a point at this location.

5. Draw a line (using a straight edge) through the two points plotted in Steps 2 and 4. The line, and all of its points, represent the infinite set of ordered pair solutions (x,y) for the linear equation $y = mx + b$.

To better illustrate the steps in the procedure, Jackie models one more equation for students. While she graphs this equation step by step, her students carefully record the steps in their own words. Jackie reminds her students to write the steps in general terms so they can use them to graph other equations (and coach their partners).

1. Beginning with the equation $2x - y = -1$, Jackie rewrites the equation in $y = mx + b$ form: $y = 2x + 1$.

2. Second, Jackie plots the y-intercept (b) on a transparency that she projects onto the board: $(0,1)$.

3. Third, she reminds students to be careful and make sure that they write the slope (m) as a fraction ($\frac{k}{h}$): $m = 2 = \frac{4}{2}$.

4. Fourth, Jackie returns to her point on the plane. She moves four units up (k) and two units to the right (h). She plots a second point here: (2,5).

5. For the fifth step in the procedure, Jackie uses a straightedge to draw a line between the two points: *line passing through (0,1) and (2,5)*.

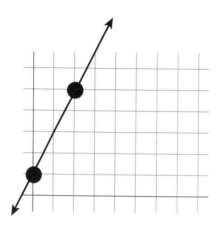

She explains to her students that for every equation of the form $y = mx + b$ there is an infinite number of ordered pairs of numbers that can be substituted for x and y to form a true equation. The set of all of the ordered pairs of numbers that make the equation true is the solution of the equation. When graphed, these points representing the solution of the equation will form a straight line.

After she finishes graphing the equation $y = 2x + 1$, Jackie organizes her students into pairs. Students share their steps with their partners and review the procedure before starting the activity together.

Jackie provides each pair of students with two equations to graph. One student puts away her steps and graphs the first equation while her partner coaches her. Students switch roles for the second equation. The student-coach from the first equation now graphs the second equation while his partner coaches him.

After all of the students have had the opportunity to graph an equation and coach their partner doing the same, Jackie brings her class back together. She asks questions and encourages her students to share their thoughts on the Proceduralizing strategy so far. Jackie wraps up her lesson by assigning students some more equations to graph for homework so they can practice using the procedure on their own.

Why the Strategy Works

Proceduralizing draws its instructional power from two distinct lines of research: direct instruction and peer coaching. Let's begin with direct instruction. Direct instruction is a broad name for those teaching frameworks that involve the teacher modeling a skill or procedure for students. After the teacher has modeled the skill, students practice it in phases, with less help and guidance from the teacher during each phase. The ultimate goal of a direct-instruction lesson is student independence.

Research has consistently shown that direct instruction has a dramatic impact on students' mathematical achievement, improving students' ability to master and retain procedures, solve problems with greater confidence, and remain focused and engaged in mathematical learning (Kroesbergen & Johannes, 2003; Flores & Kaylor, 2007).

However, we have all probably used direct instruction in our mathematics classrooms and been less than thrilled by the results. The reason for this is simple: Not all forms of direct instruction are created equal. Proceduralizing maximizes the benefits of direct instruction by adding several additions and twists to the traditional direct-instruction model. Figure 1.5 outlines these additions and twists and compares Proceduralizing to more traditional direct-instruction methods.

Traditional Methods	Proceduralizing Strategy
• Teacher models a procedure or skill.	• Teacher models a procedure or skill to the class using sample problems. • Teacher reviews the sample problems with students.
• Students copy the steps in the procedure verbatim.	• Students analyze sample problems and begin to personalize the general steps in the procedure. • Students record the steps in the procedure in their own words.
• Students are given practice problems to work on.	• Students work collaboratively in pairs to solve two problems, once by following the steps in the procedure and once by coaching their partner.
• Students can ask questions about the process.	• Students are encouraged to ask questions and share their experiences during class discussion.
• Students complete additional problems for homework.	• Students complete additional problems independently, either in class or for homework.

FIGURE 1.5 Traditional Direct Instruction Versus Proceduralizing

Of all the revisions to traditional direct instruction, the most important is the integration of a simple peer-coaching model into the larger direct-instruction framework. By allowing students to work and learn together in a structured way, you and your students reap the significant benefits associated with learning partnerships, including more on-task behavior, increased engagement, and the development of more positive attitudes towards mathematics (King-Sears & Bradley, 1995).

Planning Considerations

Mathematics contains a great number of procedures. Some procedures are more complex with numerous steps while others are more basic and contain only a few steps. Some procedures are essential to mathematics while others aren't as important and are "nice to know."

While the Proceduralizing strategy works best with critical procedures involving multiple steps, it can be used with most levels of mathematical content. When planning a Proceduralizing lesson for your classroom, you should follow these guidelines:

- *Select a procedure that maintains a high degree of consistency for a variety of problems for which the procedure applies.* For example, the procedure for finding the least common multiple (LCM) or greatest common factor (GCF) of a pair of numbers remains consistent for every pair of numbers.

- *Review prerequisite skills with students, but don't present too much information.* Most mathematical procedures rely on concepts and skills that students have learned previously. However, it is important that some time be taken to identify and review relevant concepts and skills so they do not become barriers for students. It is also important not to present so much information that the key steps in the procedure are lost.

- *Work through the procedure and generalize the steps before modeling the procedure with students.* Students are expected to generalize and record the steps of the procedure in their own words, so it is important that you have a clear set of general steps. By working through the procedure and developing a list of steps in the planning stage, you will be prepared to review the procedure, answer students' questions, and provide help and feedback as needed.

- *Make sure your examples are clear, concise, and easy to understand.* Modeling the procedure is essential to the Proceduralizing strategy. You need to consider how information will be presented to and received by students. Any written information needs to be visible and readable for all students. Manipulatives and hands-on procedures need to be easily seen and connect well to your mathematics content. Your modeling of the procedure should be clear, efficient, and, of course, mathematically accurate.

- *Allow ample time for students to write their steps in their own words, share their steps, and review the procedure with a partner.* Cognitively speaking, the most important part of the Proceduralizing activity is the period of time in which students write the steps in their own words and refine their steps with a partner.

- *Prepare appropriate problems for the cooperative learning activity.* Be sure that the problems you select are aligned with the procedure that your students are learning. Serving up problems that don't fit the procedure will deflate the entire learning experience.

Similarly, problems that are only somewhat related to the procedure can be confusing at first and should be introduced later on in the unit.

- *Select an appropriate independent practice activity to close the lesson.* Think about how you want your students to practice the procedure on their own. Assign activities for class work or homework that are meaningful and will help students further internalize the steps in the procedure.

Variations and Extensions

While the Proceduralizing strategy works best with core mathematical procedures involving multiple steps, the following moves can help you use the Proceduralizing strategy with any mathematical content.

Fill in the Blank

For younger students or students who are struggling with a procedure, you can provide students with your typed list of general steps for the procedure with a few key words missing. As students watch and study your demonstration of the procedure, they fill in the blanks of each step and capture the key elements of the procedure.

Math Vocabulary: Fun and Games

Sometimes a new mathematical procedure includes a significant number of new vocabulary words. Make sure you preview these words and define them with your students prior to starting your Proceduralizing lesson. Vocabulary games are great ways to introduce students to new and potentially intimidating terms.

Three's Company

The Proceduralizing strategy can easily work with cooperative groups of three students. After students review their steps in the procedure, they are given three problems. While one student works to solve the first problem, the other two students observe and coach using their steps. Students switch roles, so each student solves one problem and coaches twice.

Apply Technology

To verify that the procedure really does work, have students use a computer or calculator to check for themselves. For the graphs of $y = mx + b$ equations featured earlier, students could use a graphing calculator to check that their solutions and graphs are indeed correct. Also, consider using software programs to introduce your students to a procedure. A slide show is a great way to show visual representations of the procedure and reveal the steps in the procedure one at a time.

Mental Math Strings

Strategy Overview

Most math educators would agree that *in order to learn math, students must do math.* This principle, put forth by the National Council of Teachers of Mathematics (NCTM) in 1989, has served as a cornerstone for reforming mathematics instruction ever since. Today, many math educators use the term *engagement* when they talk about students doing math in the classroom.

Mental Math Strings is a daily activity that engages students directly by challenging them to call up essential facts and perform a wide variety of mathematical operations—to do math—in their heads. No calculators, no paper, no pencils. The strategy requires only a few minutes each day and can be done at the start of class, end of class, or as a break during class. We like to think of Mental Math Strings as a kind of a daily multiple vitamin for math students: They provide a rich mix of nourishing mathematical concepts and activities that help keep students' minds in peak condition.

A typical Mental Math String includes key vocabulary terms, important measurement equivalencies, and connections to important mathematical concepts. For example, a Mental Math String might contain this sequence of activities:

- Start with the number of inches in two feet.
- Add the first odd whole number to your answer.
- Divide by the number of vertices in a pentagon.
- Cube your result.
- Add the digits of your answer together.
- Multiply by the number of diagonals in a square.

So, how did you do with this Mental Math String? Did you come up with an answer of 16?

While a simple Mental Math String is beneficial to students, the daily string routine can be greatly enhanced using an instructional model called PEACE.

The progressive stages of the PEACE model ask students to

Preview the material;

Engage in the mental operations required by the string;

Assess their final answers;

Correct mistakes and errors in thinking; and

Engage in a second Mental Math String.

How to Use the Strategy

To implement Mental Math Strings in your classroom, follow the stages in the PEACE model:

Preview Stage: Preview the content, procedures, and skills embedded in the Mental Math String with your students.

Engagement Stage 1: Present the steps of the Mental Math String one at a time to students so they can compute each step in their heads.

Assessment Stage: Provide the final answer, so students can determine whether they performed all of the steps correctly.

Correction Stage: Demonstrate (verbally, in written form, or using a student volunteer) how each step is correctly performed, allowing students to identify and correct mistakes one line at a time.

Engagement Stage 2: Present a second Mental Math String that involves the same concepts, vocabulary, and procedures but uses different numbers. Collect work from all students to note and communicate rates of improvement between the first and second string.

The Strategy in Action

Joanne Ehrhardt uses Mental Math Strings to engage students in mathematical learning and continuously build their background knowledge of key vocabulary terms, measurement units, and mathematical procedures.

In the preview stage, Joanne previews the information that the students will encounter in the steps of the Mental Math String. Prior to today's Mental Math Strings challenge, Joanne asks students to activate and shore up gaps in their prior knowledge with these questions:

1. How many inches are in one foot?

2. How many inches are in one yard?

3. What is the first odd whole number?

4. What is the first even whole number?

5. How many sides are on a pentagon? On an octagon? On a hexagon?

6. How many vertices are on a pentagon? On an octagon? On a hexagon?

7. How do you square a number?

8. How do you cube a number?

9. What is the sum of the digits of the number 64? What is the product?

10. How many diagonals can be drawn on a square? On a parallelogram? On a rhombus?

The preview stage of the PEACE model provides students with opportunities to learn and review important mathematical facts and operations that will be part of the Mental Math String, along with related facts that will not explicitly appear in the string. Previewing in this way also increases students' chances of succeeding in the Mental Math Strings activity and builds students' knowledge base of critical facts and procedures.

After the preview stage, Joanne and her students enter the first engagement stage. Joanne reads each line of the Mental Math String and pauses for a few seconds after each line, giving students time to recall or determine the key number associated with that line of the string and then apply that number as an operation of the previous answer. For example, here is today's Mental Math String (Figure 1.6):

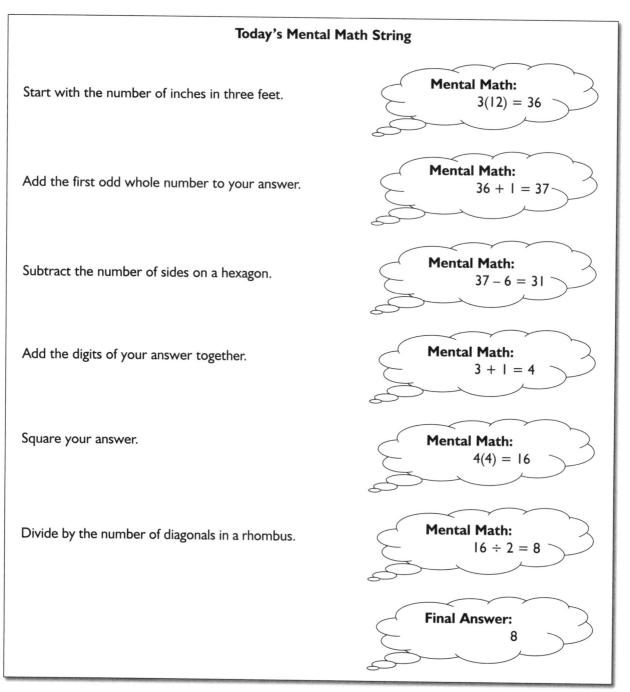

FIGURE 1.6 Today's Mental Math String

In the assessment stage that follows, Joanne invites students to turn to one another and share their final answers, and then she encourages students who feel confident about their answers to share them with the class. To alleviate any confusion or differences of opinion, Joanne quickly identifies the correct answer.

Students who did not solve the Mental Math String correctly now get an opportunity to identify what they did wrong during the correction stage of the PEACE model. To accomplish this, Joanne asks for a volunteer who solved the string correctly to stand before the class and verbally recount the steps in the string so all students can identify their mistakes one line at a time. Sometimes, the volunteer student will record the line-by-line answers on the board to make it easier for students to identify their mistakes. Joanne is always pleased by how eager students are for this opportunity to receive immediate feedback on their work. She is also very happy that the number of student moans and groans over their own mistakes and miscalculations has dropped significantly since the beginning of the year. Since using Mental Math Strings, Joanne's students are more careful, more confident, and more knowledgeable than they were at the start of the year.

During the final phase of the PEACE model, the second engagement stage, Joanne encourages students to show that they have learned from their mistakes and helps all of her students experience success. Joanne presents a second Mental Math String, which includes the same vocabulary terms and concepts as the first but contains different numbers and requires different mental calculations.

Students complete the string, check their answers, and the day's lesson begins. Before moving on to the day's lesson, however, Joanne is sure to remind students that Mental Math Strings are daily exercises and that they will work on another string tomorrow to help keep their mathematical minds sharp.

Why the Strategy Works

Some of the most striking findings in recent educational research come from studies into the power of formative assessment. For example, Robert Marzano (2006), citing a 1991 study conducted by Bangert-Drowns, Kulik, and Kulik, shows that regular formative assessment can lead to gains of 25 percentile points or more in student achievement.

So, what makes for effective formative assessment? According to Marzano, the most important criterion is "sound feedback," or feedback that

- Is frequent;
- Gives students a clear idea of how well they are learning and how they can get better; and
- Provides encouragement to the student. (Marzano, 2006, p. 11)

Mental Math Strings put the power of formative assessment and sound feedback to work in the classroom. It happens daily. It provides both the teacher and the student with good information about students' understanding of key mathematical terms and their fluency in procedures that they need to be able to perform automatically to achieve success in mathematics—all without putting undue burden on the teacher. And Mental Math Strings encourages students by giving everyone in the class the opportunity to achieve success by systematically rooting out errors in their own thinking and then putting their revised understanding to work with a second Mental Math String.

Planning Considerations

In designing Mental Math Strings, keep the following tips in mind:

1. Include terms and procedures that are central to what you're teaching. Mental Math Strings typically require general mathematical knowledge as well as more unit-specific terms and procedures. For example, the Algebra String below focuses on the terms *greatest common factor* and *coefficient*. It also requires students to apply the procedure for finding a GCF in their heads.

- Start with the greatest common factor (GCF) of 24 and 30.
- Square your result.
- Add the coefficient of $4x^5$.
- Subtract the number of degrees in a right angle.
- Square your result.

2. Keep it short and sweet. Mental Math Strings are meant to be used daily and completed quickly. Five to eight steps in a string are all you need.

3. Make two. Remember, you'll need a string for both engagement stages in the PEACE model.

4. Decide how to preview the string. Once you've identified the vocabulary, concepts, skills, and procedures students will need to know to succeed, think about what you will do to preview the activity. Will you provide questions to students as Joanne Ehrhardt did in the model lesson? Will you review and reteach the component parts? Can you involve "student-teachers" in the preview stage?

Variations and Extensions

PEACE Model

The PEACE model can be applied to any engagement activity in any mathematics classroom. Whether students are learning computation procedures with rational numbers, computing perimeters, areas, surface areas, and volumes in geometry, or solving equations in algebra, the progressive stages associated with the PEACE model will increase success rates and student learning.

The PEACE model can also be applied to homework. Students will experience more success with homework if the associated mathematical terms and procedures are previewed before students begin their homework. This might be done towards the end of class on the same day that the homework is assigned. It is equally important that the students' work is assessed the day the homework is due. Following the assessment, students should be led through the process of identifying and correcting their mistakes. Similar problems should be part of the next homework assignment so students can demonstrate that they have learned from their mistakes and can enjoy higher levels of success.

While the PEACE model described in this section includes two engagement stages, additional engagement stages can be added as needed. It is vital to the success of the strategy that the assessment and correction stages are implemented after each student engagement stage.

A final and highly engaging variation on Mental Math Strings involves student-generated strings. Challenge students to use the content they're currently learning to create Mental Math Strings for their fellow students. Students can then work in pairs or small groups to complete each other's strings, review key processes and concepts, and work through the PEACE model (or use a simplified version of the PEACE model).

Graduated Difficulty

Strategy Overview

In the mathematics classroom, students function at different levels of proficiency and comprehension. Some students may not be ready for the most challenging problems, while others become bored with problems and concepts that they have already mastered. This means that when math teachers rely on one-size-fits-all teaching and problem-solving approaches, students at both the higher and lower levels of proficiency will likely become frustrated and may disengage from the learning at hand.

The Graduated Difficulty strategy provides an effective remedy to this common classroom challenge. For a Graduated Difficulty lesson, the teacher creates three levels of problems, all representing the same math concept or skill, but at distinct levels of challenge. The first level requires students to demonstrate basic knowledge, understanding, and proficiency associated with the concept or skill. The second level includes an extension or challenge that requires students to apply their knowledge, understanding, and proficiency beyond the basic level. The third level calls for the application of higher levels of math reasoning within or even beyond the context of the math concept or skill.

Before beginning a Graduated Difficulty lesson, it is important to explain to students the value of self-assessment and to remind them that they are responsible for their choices as they

- Analyze the three tasks;
- Select the task that best fits their level of understanding;
- Complete the task and assess their performance; and
- Set goals for achievement at higher levels.

How to Use the Strategy

1. Select a math concept or skill you want your students to master.

2. Develop three problems or problem sets that represent three levels of difficulty.

3. Explain the process and the value of accomplishment associated with the varying levels of difficulty. Make sure students understand that three levels of difficulty are provided so they can analyze their own skill and comprehension levels, make choices, succeed, advance to higher levels, and get the most out their learning experience.

4. As students analyze the different problems, encourage students who are capable to select the more challenging levels, and assure all students that it's okay to begin with the easier problems and to switch levels during the activity.

5. Provide an answer key (or rubric) so students can check their work. Students who successfully complete the level three problems can

serve as coaches for other students, or they can design even more challenging problems of their own and then solve them.

6. After all the students complete their work, invite students to present their solutions to the class.

7. At the conclusion of the Graduated Difficulty activity, help students establish personal goals for improvement. Provide additional tasks or problems so students can build their knowledge, understanding, and proficiency. The additional practice can come in the form of in-class work or homework.

The Strategy in Action: Examples

Three Levels of Problem Sets Involving Integers

I. Simplify.	II. Simplify.	III. Simplify.
1. 12 – 15	1. –10 + 14 –20	1. –12 – (–20)
2. –21 + 11	2. 24 – 6 –16	2. 14 + 24 – 30
3. 32 + 14 –22	3. 12 – 30 + 15	3. –12 – 0 + 14
4. –14 – 18	4. 17 – 21 –4	4. –24 – (–20) – 11
5. –25 + 15	5. –8 + 11 – 20	5. 19 – 30 – 6 + 14

Three Levels of Word Problems Involving Percents and Discounts

Level 1: High Tech Super Store has a 25% off sale on all computers and printers. Travis bought a computer and laser printer that regularly cost $799 and $249, respectively. Disregarding tax, find the total discounted cost of the new computer and printer.

Level 2: The Johnsons are starting a new family business and need to purchase two computers and two printers. Electronics and More is having a major sale. All computers are being discounted by 25% and all printers are being discounted by 30%. Find the total discounted cost of two computers and two printers that regularly cost $899 and $299, respectively.

Level 3: Jennifer needs a new laptop computer, color ink-jet printer, and black-and-white laser printer. She also needs a new desk and chair. Computer Depot is having a sale on all its merchandise. Computers and accessories are being discounted 25%. Furniture is being discounted 40%. Find the total cost of Jennifer's purchase based on the prediscount prices shown below. Include a 6% sales tax on all items.

Laptop Computer $1199

Color Ink-Jet Printer $149

B&W Laser Printer $399

Desk $299

Chair $139

Three Levels of Geometric Problem Solving

Problem: The drawing below (Figure 1.7) consists of four circles inscribed in a square. Each circle is tangent to two other circles. The area of the square is 64 square units. Choose one of the levels below.

Level 1: Find the total area of all four circles.

Level 2: Find the area of the shaded region.

Level 3: Find the area of the hypocycloid bounded by the four circles.

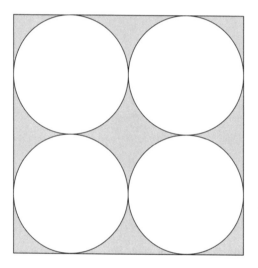

FIGURE I.7   Hypocycloid

Why the Strategy Works

Graduated Difficulty comes from the work of Muska Mosston (1972). What Mosston discovered is that when teachers invite students into the process of analyzing and selecting the work that is most appropriate for them, the classroom dynamic changes for the better. Some of the benefits include

- Increased opportunities for all learners to succeed;
- Higher levels of student engagement and focus;
- Boosts in student confidence with more students attempting higher-level tasks;
- The development of task-analysis and self-assessment skills as students work to find the best match for themselves; and
- The establishment of a collaborative culture in which teachers work with students as they reflect on and discuss their work, their decisions, and their goals.

What makes the strategy especially appealing to students is the choice. Choice is one of the strongest, most empowering of human motivators, and classrooms that encourage decision making tend to build trust between teachers and students and build students' intrinsic motivation to learn and succeed (Erwin, 2004).

The strategy is also an ideal way to develop students' goal-setting skills. As Robert Marzano's (2007) research in *The Art and Science of Teaching* shows, encouraging students to set meaningful learning goals and helping them to evaluate and track their progress leads consistently to increased achievement levels in the classroom.

Planning Considerations

The idea behind Graduated Difficulty is that students' levels of achievement can be improved by providing *options at different levels of difficulty and challenge*. Clearly, to prepare for a Graduated Difficulty lesson, you'll need to take some time to develop the three levels of problems or tasks your students will complete.

One thing to avoid when creating levels is the temptation to base difficulty on the quantity of problems you ask students to solve. Simply asking students to solve more problems doesn't lead to the kind of task analysis and self-assessment that Graduated Difficulty naturally promotes among students. In other words, basing difficulty on the number of items will not encourage students to ask questions, such as *What skills and knowledge are needed to complete each level?* and, *How do my current skills and knowledge match up to the requirements of each task?*

Figure 1.8 on page 40 shows three ways to design levels that will promote task analysis and self-assessment on the part of students.

In addition to considering how you can challenge students with three different levels of difficulty, when designing a Graduated Difficulty lesson it is important to think about the following questions.

How will you introduce and explain the lesson? Students need to understand and be comfortable with their roles in a Graduated Difficulty lesson. Make sure students know how to analyze and select a task and reinforce the idea that it is okay for students to select whichever task is the best for them. Sara Avery, a middle school mathematics teacher, designed a poster (Figure 1.9) to help students through her Graduated Difficulty lessons.

How will students check their work? Students should be able to self-assess their work to determine if they have arrived at a correct answer and have made a good choice. To help students determine if they have completed their chosen task correctly and well, provide them with an answer key that shows how the answer was calculated. For more open-ended activities, you might choose to give students a rubric with clear guidelines and benchmarks.

How will students reflect on their learning? The ultimate goal of Graduated Difficulty is to help all students move to higher levels of thinking and learning. It is important for students to take stock of where they are

Level of	What It Means	Examples
Rigor of Content	Basing levels on the degree of rigor or the depth of knowledge needed to complete each level.	*Scenario 1:* A middle school math teacher provides three levels of equations to solve. At the first level, all equations take the form $ax + b = c$. The second level adds equations in the form $a(x + b) + c = d$, while the third level adds equations in the form $a(x + b) + c = d(x + e)$. *Scenario 2:* While teaching geometry, a teacher might provide three levels of surface area problems. The three levels might differ according to the complexity of the figures as shown. (Each figure requires the knowledge and application of additional operations.) **Level 1** **Level 2** **Level 3**
Support or Given Information Provided	Basing the levels on the degree of support or background information provided in the task.	As part of the class's work with mathematical properties (commutative, associative, distributive, and identity), a teacher provides three levels of tasks. With each level, the amount of given information decreases. • At Level 1, the names of the properties and a set of equations are given. Students have to identify the property or properties illustrated in each equation. • At Level 2, the names of the properties are given. Students have to create an equation illustrating each property. • At Level 3, students are given neither names nor equations. They have to create a table that includes the name of each property, an equation that illustrates it, and a simple explanation of how each equation illustrates each property.
Thinking Process	Basing levels on the sophistication of thinking required by each task.	For a task involving data analysis (for example, two graphs with one showing the number of U.S. farms from 1950 to the present day and another showing the size in acres of the average farm over the same span), you might create your levels by • Asking students to describe the data at Level 1 (What do the two graphs show?); • Asking students to find patterns at Level 2 (How do the two charts relate to each other mathematically? What conclusions can you make?); and • Asking students to make and explain predictions at Level 3 (What do you think the charts will show in the year 2025? How about 2100? What evidence would you use to support your predictions?).

FIGURE 1.8 How to Create Different Kinds of Graduated Tasks

Self-assess your current level of understanding about the content or skill to be practiced.

Examine the different levels of difficulty, and choose the level that is appropriate for you.

Look over your work and adjust if necessary by attempting a different level of activity or challenging yourself by creating a more difficult activity.

Evaluate the criteria you used to make your initial choice.

Consider your decision by asking: Did I choose the right level for me?

Take time to establish a personally meaningful goal for improvement.

FIGURE 1.9 SELECT Graduated Difficulty Poster

at the end of the lesson so they can chart their own goals for improvement. To help students develop personal learning goals, encourage them to share their work and decision-making process with others through classroom discussion and teacher conferences. Think about how you will help students convey their thoughts and experiences with questions like these:

- What went well for you in this lesson?
- What caused you trouble?
- What criteria would you use to examine your choice and work?
- Do you think you made the right choice?
- What do you need to do to move to a higher level?

Variations and Extensions

The Graduated Difficulty strategy can be implemented with the following variations and extensions.

- Depending on the complexity of the problems students will be solving, you may choose to implement the Paired Learner model (see pages 150–158) and allow students to work in pairs. This will encourage teamwork, communication, and collaboration among students.
- The teacher can select students or pairs of students and provide them with transparencies so they can easily share their work with the class during the presentation of solutions.
- Students who have higher levels of understanding and proficiency can be encouraged and rewarded for completing all three levels of problems successfully.

New American Lecture

Strategy Overview

Mathematics is filled with content and procedures that students need to remember if they are going to succeed. For teachers, this raises a critical question: How can we make the information we present in the classroom more engaging and more memorable? New American Lecture provides a mathematics teacher with a strategic way of delivering content and providing direct instruction in a mathematical procedure. In a typical New American Lecture, the teacher provides students with four kinds—or Ps—of support:

- The teacher *prepares* students for the lecture with an engaging hook.
- The teacher *presents* brief chunks of content, which students record on a visual organizer.
- The teacher *pauses* after each chunk and poses a review question.
- The teacher provides time for students to *process* content and/or *practice* skills during and after the lecture.

How to Use the Strategy

Developing and implementing a New American Lecture requires 4 Ps:

1. Prepare a hook. Prepare a way to "hook" student interest and involve them in the content. Open discussion with a topic-related question, but with a question that may appear to be off the wall. Encourage students to think and share responses in small groups; then, open up a class discussion.

2. Present the content in chunks using a visual organizer. Chunks are subsets of the material that will either overlap or subsequently be connected to other chunks of the content.

3. Pause every 5 minutes. Pause periodically throughout instruction to ask students to think about the content in multiple ways, from different perspectives.

4. Process and/or practice the material. Assess the nature of content:
   a. If declarative content, provide focused time for students to process the material; or
   b. If procedural content, provide appropriate practice materials and class time.

The Strategy in Action

Alan Gorman teaches algebra. Today, Alan is using New American Lecture to teach his students about three common transformations: translations, reflections, and dilations.

Phase One: Prepare Students for Learning

Alan begins the lesson by asking students if they've seen any of the *Transformers* movies. "What do you know about Transformers? Why are they called Transformers?" Alan asks. After students offer their ideas, Alan explains that Transformers help illustrate a critical concept in mathematics: transformation.

Alan provides students with a simple definition of transformation and then helps students brainstorm some real-world examples, including

- Changing an assigned seat in the classroom;
- Changing lanes while driving;
- Changing the size of a photograph or computer graphic; and
- Changing direction while dancing.

With each new example, Alan asks students to think about two questions: One, What does each type of change look like? and two, What does each change feel like? Then, to focus students' attention on the specific content of the lecture, Alan asks students to describe, in words, the actual or apparent change in their physical position or size if they:

- Took one step backward (translation);
- Looked in a full-length mirror (reflection); and
- Viewed a 3×5 picture of themselves (dilation).

After the discussion, Alan connects students' ideas to the lesson by saying,

It turns out that our three scenarios that we've been discussing—taking a step backward, looking in a mirror, and viewing a photograph—are examples of the three most common types of transformations, which are called translation, reflection, and dilation. Of course, in mathematics, we can describe these kinds of changes in position and size with perfect precision and in more than one way. By the end of today's lesson, you will be able to describe translation, reflection, and dilation in four different ways: verbally in your own words, visually by sketching each transformation, algebraically by representing each transformation as an equation, and by identifying your own real-world example of each.

Phase Two: Present the Content

Alan distributes a visual organizer designed around the three transformations. For each transformation, students have to make notes that define the transformation, then show it visually, represent it algebraically, and cite at least one real-world example. A student's partially completed organizer looks like Figure 1.10 on page 44.

Phase Three: Pause Every 5 Minutes

Each type of transformation represents one chunk of the lecture, and each takes roughly five minutes to present. After each 5-minute segment, Alan stops lecturing, gives his students an extra minute or 2 to complete

A *transformation is* _a change in position or size of a geometric figure_

	Translation	Reflection	Dilation
Define	Slide a figure without turning it, preserves size and shape.	Flip a figure over a line, creating mirror image preserves size and shape.	
Visualize			
Algebraic	Given $y = f(x)$ $y_1 = f(x+h)$ or $y_2 = f(x) + K$		
Real-World Examples	sliding glass door		

FIGURE 1.10 Student's Partially Completed Organizer

their notes, and then poses a question to help students think more deeply about transformations and how to apply them. To engage all his learners and to help students develop greater perspective and understanding of the content, Alan rotates the styles of the questions he poses.

After the first chunk on translations, Alan asks a Mastery question designed to help students practice and review what they learned: *In terms of an arbitrary function f(x), can you algebraically define g(x), a horizontal translation of eight units?*

After the second chunk on reflections, Alan poses an Understanding question focused on comparative analysis: *Compare and contrast translations and reflections. What is similar and different about them algebraically, graphically, and numerically?*

After the third chunk on dilation, Alan poses an Interpersonal question focused on real-world applications of the three transformations: *Many careers, especially those involving design, use transformations as part of the planning and creative process. Think of a career activity that might use these three types of transformations (e.g., architect, artist, graphic designer, etc.). Describe or illustrate how all three types of transformations might be part of the career activity.*

Finally, after all of the transformation types have been presented, Alan poses a Self-Expressive question focused on visualizing and applying the three transformations: *Choose one of our unit's vocabulary words and print the letters of that word in block form on graph paper. On the same or on separate graphs, translate, dilate, and reflect the vocabulary word. Be sure to label each transformation and describe its changes from your original.*

Phase Four: Practice/Process

For the final phase of the New American Lecture, Alan wants to help students develop mastery over the skill of graphing and describing transformations. So, he provides a set of practice activities including the activity shown below.

1. Using the function $f(x) = y = |x + 2|$,

    a. Graph, label, and describe the transformation $y_1 = f(x + 3)$
    b. Graph, label, and describe the transformation $y_2 = f(-x)$
    c. Graph, label, and describe the transformation $y_3 = 2f(x)$

But Alan knows that "following the procedures" is not enough when it comes to understanding mathematics deeply. So, after students have completed the activities, he presents them with a task that requires them to explain how transformations work numerically and to use their explanations to make mathematical predictions: *For each type of transformation, explain how knowing the value of the constant, in each transformation's algebraic form, enables you to predict the pattern of change that will be seen in a corresponding set of numerical data. Use a sketch to support your explanation.*

Why the Strategy Works

The effectiveness of the New American Lecture is tied directly to the four Ps of support that it provides to students.

First, the teacher *prepares* students for the lecture using a hook. A good hook primes the engine for deep learning by engaging students' curiosity and activating students' prior knowledge. There are four different kinds, or styles, of hooks.

1. Mastery hooks ask students to recall information.

2. Understanding hooks ask students to use logic and reasoning to analyze an issue or controversy.

3. Self-Expressive hooks ask students to call on their imagination.

4. Interpersonal hooks ask students to draw on their personal experiences.

Examples of each of these styles of hooks are shown in Figure 1.13 (on page 49). To connect the students' ideas that emerge in response to the hook, the teacher then bridges those responses to the content of the lecture with a simple statement that sounds like this: "These are some wonderful ideas you've generated. Now let's see how your ideas relate to _____."

For the second P of support, the teacher *presents* the content of the lecture using a visual organizer. This P actually contains two distinct supports. First, content is presented in brief three to five minute chunks. Chunking information by breaking it into manageable pieces facilitates processing and increases the likelihood of moving that information into long-term memories where it can be recalled when needed (Gobet, et al., 2001). The second support contained within this P is the visual organizer. The visual organizer shows how all the chunks in the lecture fit together to form a whole. And as Hyerle (2000) has noted, organizers also foster an evolution in students' thinking processes: First, they learn how to manage information, and then they learn how to actively construct new knowledge.

The third P of support, *pause* every 3 to 5 minutes to pose a review question, gives students the opportunity to play with, refine, and shore up gaps in their learning. As with chunking, review questions deepen processing and help students turn the new information into long-term memories. To help students examine the content deeply and from multiple perspectives, you should rotate the kinds of questions you ask during your lectures. Figure 1.12 (page 48) shows you how to use learning styles to design and pose different kinds of questions.

The final P serves double duty. If the lecture is more declarative in nature, (e.g., famous number patterns) students will need an opportunity to further *process* the content by putting their learning to work by completing a task or creating a product. If the lecture is more procedural or skill based (e.g., how to solve problems using slope-intercept form), students will need the opportunity to *practice* their new skills.

Planning Considerations

Identify Your Topic

In mathematics, it is usually easy to select a topic, but you need to collect and chunk all of the information that you anticipate students will be learning. As you think of the topic, jot down all of the words that come into your mind. Be sure to include words, processes, or theorems that connect this topic to past mathematics.

Once you have all of the information, fit it all together. Create information chunks, or subgroups of information, by identifying the key words within the topic. These chunks will help you create a visual organizer and suggest the logical and important instructional breaks in your lecture.

Design the Visual Organizer

A good visual organizer will help students see the whole as the sum of its parts, how small bits of information come together to form a larger picture. Given your topic and its information chunks, you can design a visual organizer that both guides you and supports your students' learning during the lecture. A visual organizer should highlight your topic's key conceptual patterns and help scaffold learning. Figure 1.11 shows a variety of organizers highlighting common mathematical conceptual patterns.

Develop Review Questions

Information chunks provide opportunities for students to deal with manageable amounts of content. Plan to present these chunks in roughly

Concept Definition Organizer
Fancy Number Sequences

Concept	Definition	Math/Visual Illustration
Pascal's Triangle		
Fibonacci Sequence		
Golden Ratio		

Acronym Organizer

Multiplying Polynomials	
F	
O	
I	
L	

Comparative Organizer

Surface Area	Volume

Similarities

Topic Organizer

Systems of Equations - Solution Methods

Graphing	Elimination	Substitution	Determinants
Details	Details	Details	Details

Matrix Organizer

Prism	Shape of base	# base sides	# prism vertices	# prism faces	# prism edges
triangular					
rectangular					
pentagonal					
hexagonal					
octagonal					

Sequence Organizer

Start →

Verify your work by substituting for (x).

Solve for (x).

Simplify the equation.

Eliminate square roots by squaring both sides.

Look at problem and set up equation.

Principle Organizer

Property	Explanation	Math/Visual Representation	Application
associative			
commutative			
transitive			

FIGURE 1.11 A Potpourri of Visual Organizers for Mathematics

5-minute intervals of lecture. Plan to stop after each lecture chunk to pose questions that will facilitate processing and require students to recall and use what they just learned. Strive to use a variety of question types during the lecture to stimulate different ways of thinking about the content. Learning styles represent one of the most effective and manageable models for incorporating a variety of questions into your teaching. Figure 1.12 below shows how the four styles of questions can be adapted to mathematical content.

Design the Hook

A hook is a designed question or activity that attracts student interest, focuses thinking, and opens memory banks closely associated with the new topic. Sometimes, a hook may appear to have little to do with mathematics. To create a hook, think deeply about your topic and the words that you first

Mastery questions ask students to	*Interpersonal questions ask students to*
Recall and Practice	*Make Real-World Connections*
• Can you remember the steps in the procedure for solving proportion problems?	• Can you think of three activities or situations in which accuracy of measurement is critical?
Restate	*Personalize Learning*
• Cover your organizer. How much can you remember about the commutative property? Restate it.	• What information from this lecture seems most difficult to you? Why?
Summarize	*Make Value-Based Decisions*
• What is a line of best fit? Summarize in your own words.	• Which form of graphing do you like best? Why is it your favorite?
Understanding questions ask students to	*Self-Expressive questions ask students to*
Compare and Contrast	*Explore Metaphors*
• What are the key similarities and differences between prime and composite numbers?	• How is measuring circumference like running on a track?
Prove or Disprove	*Use Visuals and Symbols*
• Argue for or against this statement: The United States should convert to the metric system.	• Create an icon or sketch that represents surface area and another that represents volume.
Explain	*Ask "What If?"*
• Why can't we ever put a zero in the denominator?	• What if there were no such thing as order of operations? What would happen?

FIGURE 1.12 Four Styles of Review Questions

Source: Adapted from Thoughtful Education Press (2007). *Questioning Styles and Strategies: How to Use Questions to Engage and Motivate Different Styles of Learners.*

Mastery Hook (Focuses on Remembering)	**Interpersonal Hook** (Focuses on Personal Experiences)
Take one minute to think about everything you know about the metric system. What do you already know about this system and how it's used? *Bridge:* Good! You know quite a bit about the metric system. Now, let's build some new information on top of what you already know.	Have you ever found the English system difficult to work with (e.g., measuring small things, following a recipe)? What happened? Can you describe the difficulty you experienced? *Bridge:* Great! You've actually described some of the reasons that led to the development of the metric system. Let's investigate further to see what else we can learn.
Understanding Hook (Focuses on Reasoning)	**Self-Expressive Hook** (Focuses on Imaginative Thinking)
We use the English system in the United States, but our doctors and scientists use the metric system. Why do you think this is the case? *Bridge:* You have some good ideas! Now, let's see which of our ideas are true by investigating some of the advantages of the metric system.	What if the United States converted to the metric system tomorrow? How might your life change? *Bridge:* Super! You've generated a list of ways life might be more difficult. Now, let's look at some of the ways life might become easier.

FIGURE 1.13   Four Hooks and Bridges for a Lesson on the Metric System

generated. What mathematics concept is embedded within? How does this concept show itself in the real world, in the student's world? Does it appear in the music, art, communication, or other interests of your students? As with your review questions, you may want to use learning styles to create different kinds of hooks and promote different styles of thinking for different lectures. Figure 1.13 shows four different ways of beginning a lecture on the metric system. Notice how each style of hook gets students to think about the content to come in a different way. Which one would you choose for you classroom?

Variations and Extensions

Visual Organizers

Visual organizers are much more than supplemental forms for students to make notes and collect ideas. Visual organizers are great learning tools that, if designed thoughtfully, can shape a lesson, give structure to a difficult reading or word problem, and reinforce important ideas and connections for students that might otherwise be lost. The educational benefits of visual organizers have been widely reported by David Hyerle (2000) and others. Teach students how to use and create simple visual organizers that will serve them in the mathematics classroom. Some of the best and most common organizers for the study of mathematics were discussed earlier in Planning Considerations (see Figure 1.11 on page 47).

2

Understanding Strategies

OVERVIEW

Understanding strategies help students uncover and explain the principles and big ideas behind the mathematics they study.

Understanding math students . . .

- *Want to* understand why the math they learn works.
- *Like math problems that* ask them to explain, prove, or take a position.
- *Approach problem solving* by looking for patterns and identifying hidden questions.
- *Experience difficulty when* there is a focus on the social environment of the classroom (e.g., on collaboration and cooperative problem solving).
- *Want a math teacher who* challenges them to think and who lets them explain their thinking.

The four Understanding strategies in this chapter can help you meet these NCTM Process Standards.

Strategy	NCTM Process Standards*				
	Problem Solving	Reasoning and Proof	Communication	Connections	Representation
Reading for Meaning [p. 52] Students analyze statements about a word problem, scenario, or text and make predictions before reading, collect evidence to support or refute each statement during reading, and draw conclusions after reading.	✔		✔		
Compare and Contrast [p. 60] Students compare and contrast two concepts, procedures, or word problems by describing each using criteria, comparing both using a visual organizer, drawing conclusions about their ideas, and applying what they've learned.	✔		✔		✔
Concept Attainment [p. 70] Students examine the critical attributes of examples and nonexamples to identify a core concept.				✔	✔
Math Busters [p. 76] Students use their knowledge of mathematics to test a claim; students identify a claim, develop a hypothesis, collect data, make calculations, draw conclusions, and present their findings.		✔	✔	✔	

FIGURE 2.0   Correlation of Understanding Strategies to NCTM Process Standards

*For more information on the National Council of Teachers of Mathematics (NCTM) Process Standards, please consult their *Principles and Standards for School Mathematics* (2000), or visit their website at www.nctm.org.

Reading for Meaning

Strategy Overview

Mathematics classrooms incorporate more innovative textbooks and supplemental materials than ever before; so, for students to be proficient and successful in mathematics, they must be able to read these rich texts well (Draper, 2002). If that's not reason enough to incorporate reading strategies into your mathematics classroom, here's another: "The ability to read mathematically is essential in today's climate of high-stakes testing. Many of the questions designed to test mathematics skills are word problems, which require the test taker to read the problem, comprehend what they are expected to do and then choose and execute some mathematical algorithm" (Carter & Dean, 2006, p. 130). The pressing question before math teachers is, then, *How can we help all students develop a strategic approach to mathematical reading without taking valuable focus away from the content itself?*

Reading for Meaning helps teachers of mathematics answer this critical question. In a Reading for Meaning lesson, students are given simple statements (which can be either true, false, or open to interpretation) that force them to think carefully about a mathematical text or word problem. For example, imagine a short textbook reading explaining the rules of probability that govern the multistate lottery known as Powerball. Now, imagine that before the reading, students are presented with four statements on an organizer that looks like Figure 2.1:

Evidence For	Statements	Evidence Against
	1. There is only one way to win the grand Powerball prize.	
	2. Simple multiplication is all you need to know to calculate your odds of winning Powerball.	
	3. The odds of winning the grand prize with one ticket are 1 in 146,107,962.	
	4. The odds of a grand prizewinner living in Pennsylvania are greater than the odds of the winner living in Idaho.	

FIGURE 2.1   Powerball Reading for Meaning Organizer

What these statements and organizer do is engage students in three distinct and active phases of learning. Before reading, students preview the statements, call up relevant prior knowledge, and use that knowledge to make predictions about the text. During reading, they search for information and evidence that supports or refutes each statement. After reading, students look back on what they have learned and reflect on how their initial ideas have changed or evolved.

The Reading for Meaning strategy also builds the habits of mind associated with good mathematical problem solvers. It teaches students to slow down their thinking, form and support hypotheses, and explain their interpretations using the language of mathematics.

How to Use the Strategy

1. Provide students with a set of four to eight Reading for Meaning statements that highlight essential elements in a mathematics reading and a Reading for Meaning organizer with space to collect evidence. Depending on your objectives, you can ask students to:

- *Decide whether they agree or disagree with the statements.* This works well when the statements are general enough for students to make educated guesses about them. For example, with statements such as *To run in a line means to run straight* and *A line and a circle can have just a single point in common*, students can use their background knowledge of circles and lines to form meaningful guesses about the truth of these statements.

- *Preview the statements and predict what the reading or problem will be about.* Sometimes statements are too specific for students to do anything other than guess blindly at their truth (for example, a statement such as *An advantage of the intercept form of the line is that both the x and y intercepts of the graph are revealed*). In this case, students can look over all the statements and form a prediction about the reading as a whole.

2. Instruct students to collect evidence as they read that either supports or refutes each statement. Evidence should be recorded in either the Evidence For or Evidence Against column of a Reading for Meaning organizer.

3. After reading, have students meet with other students to discuss their findings and seek agreement on whether the evidence supports or refutes each statement. Students should also discuss what the reading taught them.

4. Conduct a whole-class discussion in which students share their take on each statement and the evidence they gathered to support their positions.

5. Extend the learning by having students develop a summary or complete a task.

The Strategy in Action

A Fish Problem

Caitlin Shea was concerned with her students' tendency to be careless or impetuous when solving word problems. In response, she began using Reading for Meaning to slow her students down and help them pay attention to facts, focus on the questions to be answered, and think about potential problem-solving approaches—all before solving the word problem. For example, Caitlin gave her students this word problem (Figure 2.2) along with the following set of statements.

Problem		
A rectangular fish tank holds 50.8 liters of water. The tank will contain just one type of goldfish and that type of goldfish grows to a length of 10 centimeters and may live for up to 3 years. If each fish requires 2.4 liters of water, how many goldfish can live in the tank?		
Evidence For	**Statements**	**Evidence Against**
	1. The problem tells us the volume of the fish tank.	
	2. Solving the problem requires us to determine the measurements of the fish tank.	
	3. The average length of a single goldfish is irrelevant to answering the question.	
	4. A spherical fish tank, also holding 50.8 liters of water, could hold just as many goldfish.	

FIGURE 2.2 Fish Problem and Statements

After students read the problem and the statements, they begin to use the statements to analyze the demands of the problem. Using the Evidence For and Evidence Against columns, students collect information from the problem or develop a simple explanation that shows the statement to be true or false. For example, for the third statement, one student wrote the following in the Evidence For column:

We don't have to worry about the length of the goldfish. All we need to know about each goldfish is how many liters of water it needs.

Once students have completed their organizers, they use their findings to solve the problem. Then, students compare their analyses and problem-solving processes with other students in small groups. Caitlin surveys different groups' interpretations and problem-solving processes, and she uses this student input to lead the class in a discussion of how using statements improves problem solving.

During the discussion, students compare this problem to other similar problems they've solved. To synthesize what they've learned, students develop a volume problem of their own, along with a set of statements that will help another student break down and solve their problem.

Geometry and Art

Adrian Merchant is introducing the topic of geometric translations to his students. His textbook has a wonderful reading on geometry and the art of M. C. Escher, which provides students with some biographical information about Escher and offers insight into how he created intricate drawings by starting with simple geometric translations and tessellations.

Adrian has designed a Reading for Meaning activity to help his students read the text carefully and connect geometric translations to their own creative and artistic interests. Here are Adrian's Reading for Meaning statements:

1. A *translation* is a geometric figure moved from one place to another without turning it.

2. A jigsaw puzzle with pieces of various sizes would be an example of a *tessellation*.

3. Translation and tessellation play important roles in M. C. Escher's art.

4. M. C. Escher is more of a mathematician than an artist.

5. I can draw a pattern unit that has a parallelogram as the basic tessellation.

After students preview the statements, collect evidence from the text that either confirms or calls into question each statement, and discuss their findings in small groups, Adrian has them apply their learning by creating their own tessellating patterns.

Why the Strategy Works

Not too many years ago, reading instruction and mathematics instruction lived in their own separate worlds and had very little to do with one another. Now, both research and classroom practice have helped correct this unnatural separation of math and literacy. We now know that students of mathematics must be readers of mathematics. State tests, with their emphasis on word problems, demand it. But more than that, we now know that good math instruction must be about more than teaching procedures. Students need to master the vocabulary and the concepts of mathematics; they must become fluent in the *language* of mathematics. Here's how Thomasenia Adams (2003), an expert on mathematics and literacy instruction, puts it:

> The words, symbols, and numerals that give the discipline its substance, framework, and power are the same words, symbols, and numerals that students must use to communicate ideas, perform procedures, explain processes, and solve problems. Hence a knower of mathematics is a doer of mathematics, and a doer of mathematics is a reader of mathematics. (p. 794)

This is one reason why the National Council of Teachers of Mathematics (2000) encourages all teachers of mathematics to incorporate reading and reading strategies into their classrooms. It's also why the NCTM argues for communication-rich mathematics classrooms in which students clarify, refine, and consolidate their thinking through listening, reading, writing, and speaking.

Reading for Meaning takes the best research on reading and literacy instruction and puts it to work in the mathematics classroom. It divides the learning into three distinct phases because research shows that effective readers outperform average and below-average readers by interacting with the text in three distinct phases (Pressley, 2006). During prereading, students use their prior knowledge and the Reading for Meaning statements to make predictions about what the text will reveal. As they read, students search actively for evidence that confirms or challenges their predictions. After reading, students review the state of their learning and work with other students to negotiate their ideas and explain their thinking and interpretations.

Best of all, you can achieve a variety of learning objectives through Reading for Meaning. As you'll see in the planning section, you can craft statements that help students develop their problem-solving skills, deepen their understanding of key concepts, build their ability to analyze and explain data, and develop their capacity to visualize abstract ideas, among others.

Planning Considerations

Without a doubt, the most important elements in a Reading for Meaning lesson are the statements themselves. Statements have the power to hook student attention, generate curiosity, redirect thinking, and establish a reading focus. Before creating your statements, think about the big ideas and key information you want your students to learn, the "chunks" of information you want to highlight, and the prior knowledge you expect students to activate.

These three questions represent a set of general guidelines for thinking about your statements. When crafting your lesson, try to incorporate a variety of statements to help your students stretch and improve their critical reading skills.

Indeed, one of the greatest powers of Reading for Meaning comes from the way in which you can craft statements to address specific mathematical challenges your students face as problem solvers and as readers of mathematical texts.

Planning Word-Problem-Based Reading for Meaning Lessons

Let's begin by looking at statements that improve students' problem solving skills, using this word problem as a model:

> At 11:00 pm eastern time, a jet leaves Cheyenne for Pittsburgh traveling at 600 miles per hour. One hour later, at midnight eastern time, a different jet leaves Pittsburgh for Cheyenne, traveling at 700 miles per hour. The first jet cruises at 10,000 feet while the second jet travels at 12,000 feet. The distance between Pittsburgh and Cheyenne is 1,427 miles. At what time do the two jets pass each other?

In designing your statements to help students analyze and solve the problem, you can craft statements that will focus students' attention on

The facts of the problem

Sample statement: The two jets are traveling in opposite directions.

The questions (and hidden questions) within the problem

Sample statement: The first jet is almost halfway to Pittsburgh when the second jet takes off.

Sample statement: It is important to know that both jets are traveling after midnight.

The problem-solving process

Sample statement: The best way to solve the problem is by setting up a time-distance-rate equation.

The solution

Sample statement: The answer to the problem will be a time of day.

Planning Text-Based Reading for Meaning Lessons

Now, let's look at the different types of statements we can use to help students overcome the most common challenges associated with reading and interpreting mathematical ideas and texts. Well-crafted Reading for Meaning statements can help students to

Visualize mathematical ideas

Sample statement: A good geometric representation of a plane is the top of your desk.

Understand mathematical vocabulary and concepts

Sample statement: When perpendicular lines intersect, they always form a right angle.

Find main ideas

Sample statement: A good headline for the reading would be, "It's Not Worth the Trouble to Convert to the Metric System."

Take a position

Sample statement: The *mean* is the most reliable indicator of central tendency.

Interpret mathematical data

Sample statement: Based on the chart, it's safe to assume that 50% of the world's energy will come from renewable sources by 2050.

Make real-world connections

Sample statement: Using a map to figure out how far you are from New York City requires an understanding of ratio.

Connect mathematics to other disciplines

Sample statement: Point of convergence is probably an important concept for most artists.

Develop a personal perspective

Sample statement: Life would be harder if Pythagoras had never developed his famous theorem.

Variations and Extensions

Once students have had experience supporting and refuting teacher-generated Reading for Meaning statements, you can have students preread an assignment and generate their own set of statements to be exchanged with other students. To avoid a common tendency to write superficial statements, consider asking students to write statements that are verifiable by answering at least one hidden question, that require some important prior knowledge, or that call for inference and deep thinking.

Also, remember that mathematics is not only embedded in readings and complex word problems but also in relatively simple looking, symbolic mathematical statements. A well-designed set of Reading for Meaning statements can help students unlock and unpack the mathematical riches in symbolic or visual representations. For example, given the statement, *Quadrilateral RSTU is congruent to quadrilateral GDQC,* you can ask students whether they agree or disagree with the statements given below (Figure 2.3). Then, have students seek to provide "proof" of their position using theorems or counterexamples.

Agree	Statement	Disagree
	1. $\angle R \cong \angle DGC$	
	2. $\angle R \cong \angle DQG$	
	3. $\angle RST \cong \angle QDR$	
	4. $\overline{ST} \cong \overline{DQ}$	
	5. $\overline{RT} \cong \overline{GC}$	
	6. $\triangle STR \cong \triangle DQC$	
	7. Area of quadrilateral $RSTU$ = area of quadrilateral $CQDG$	

FIGURE 2.3   Quadrilateral Reading for Meaning Statements

Compare and Contrast

Strategy Overview

Mathematics is an abstract language, and much of the content we teach can be abstract (impossible to see, hear, smell, taste, or touch) or easily mixed up with other ideas. To avoid the learning pitfalls associated with the abstract and easily confused elements in our content area, we need to increase students' ability to "see" the content they are learning. For example, if you want students to understand linear relationships, you can effectively double student insight into linear relationships by setting non-linear relationships against them. By placing side by side two ideas that share some critical aspects and that have other critical aspects that are unique, we can enhance students' comprehension of both concepts at the same time.

We have all probably experienced a time in our teaching when a comparison strategy did not result in deeper understanding of a topic or concept. The question we have to ask ourselves then, is, "If making comparisons is so powerful, what can we do to improve the effect that comparative thinking has on student learning in our mathematics classrooms?" The answer can be found by leading students through a four-phase process in which they:

- Describe each topic or concept separately before conducting a comparison;
- Identify similarities and differences using a visual organizer;
- Draw and discuss conclusions; and
- Apply what they learned by completing a meaningful synthesis task.

How to Use the Strategy

1. Select two (or more) related terms, concepts, or problems.

2. Specify criteria for comparison.

3. Provide (or teach students how to create) graphic organizers for describing items and comparing them. (See Organizers B and C on pages 68 and 69 for reproducible templates.)

4. Guide students through the four phases of comparison:
   - Description Phase
     - Establish a purpose for the comparison.
     - Identify sources of relevant information.

○ Clarify the criteria for describing items.

○ Have students describe the two items using a Description Organizer (see Organizer B on page 68).

- Comparison Phase
  ○ Provide students with a Comparison Organizer (see Organizer C on page 69).
  ○ Have students use the organizer to identify and collect key similarities and differences.

- Conclusion Phase
  ○ Ask students to decide if the two items are more alike or more different.
  ○ Explore and discuss some causes and effects of the differences.
  ○ Help students form generalizations.

- Application Phase
  ○ Present students with a new problem or task.
  ○ Have students apply their learning to the new problem or task.

The Strategy in Action

Helena Karras is using Compare and Contrast to help students analyze the subtle differences found in time-distance-rate problems and to master the procedure for solving them. Let's listen in on her classroom.

"Today, we are going to do two things. First, we are going to introduce a new kind of word problem, namely time-distance-rate problems." (Note that Helena reviews the formula d = r • t and the terms with students.) "Second, we are going to use a strategy called *Compare and Contrast* to help us learn how to read word problems more analytically so that we know exactly what the problem is asking us to do before we try to solve it."

Description Phase

"Here are two word problems. Using the organizer, I want you to describe what each problem is asking you to do and draw a diagram showing each problem situation. You're also going to solve the problem, showing both the answer and the steps you followed to solve the problem on your organizer." (Figure 2.4 on page 62 shows a completed organizer.)

Problem One: Samuel is running late for a meeting in Cortville, which is 40 miles down Route 27. Samuel is supposed to be at his meeting by 4:00 PM. It is now 3:15 PM. The speed limit on Route 27 is 35 miles per hour. If Samuel drives exactly 35 miles per hour, how late will he be?

Problem Two: Samuel is running late again! This time his meeting is down Breward Parkway. The meeting is 40 miles away and it is now 3:15 PM. If Samuel needs to be at his meeting by 4:00 PM, how fast will he have to drive?

	Problem 1	**Problem 2**
How is the problem written? (What needs to be found out?)	The problem is asking me to figure out when Samuel will arrive. Once I figure out how long he will be driving, I can figure out how late he will be.	The problem is asking me to figure out Samuel's rate of speed. This is the "r" in the formula.
What does the diagram look like?	Leaves at 3:15pm Arrives at ? 35 mph 40 miles	Leaves at 3:15pm Arrives at 4.00pm ? mph 40 miles
What is the answer to the problem?	24 minutes	53 miles per hour
How did you go about solving the problem? (Describe your thinking process.)	The formula is $d = r \cdot t$ The distance is 40 miles. The rate is 35 mph. $40 = 35 \cdot t$ $t = 1.143$ hours which you have to convert into approximately 69 minutes. This means that Samuel will arrive at 4:24pm, or 24 minutes late.	The formula is $d = r \cdot t$ The distance is 40 miles. The time is 45 minutes. The time needs to be converted into hours since rate is miles per hour. Converted time is .75 hours. So, $40 = r \cdot .75$, then rate is 53.33 or approximately 53 miles per hour.

FIGURE 2.4   Student's Comparative Problem-Solving Organizer

Comparison Phase

"Next, let's compare the two problems. Using the criteria from the description phase, complete the comparison organizer" (Figure 2.5).

Problem 1	Problem 2
Rate (r) is given. Time (t) is missing. The problem asks me to find out how late Samuel will be. The answer needs to be in minutes.	Time (t) is given, but needs to be calculated using the start and end times. Rate (r) is missing. The problem asks me to find out how fast Samuel needs to drive. The answer will be in miles per hour (mph).
Similarities	
Both problems use the time-distance-rate formula (d = r • t). Both problems involve the time it takes to travel somewhere by car. Both problems give the distance. Both diagrams look similar. Both problems require converting time into hours or minutes.	

FIGURE 2.5 Student's Comparison Organizer

Conclusion Phase

"With your partner, develop a brief that explains your findings. Be sure to discuss what causes the differences in how you go about solving each type of problem."

Application Phase

"To show what you know, create two problems like problem one and two problems like problem two. Then, since we noticed that problem one asks you to solve for time and problem two asks you to solve for rate, create two more problems that are looking for you to solve for distance."

Why the Strategy Works

By analyzing a wide body of research on effective classroom strategies, McREL researchers Robert Marzano, Debra Pickering, and Jane Pollock (2001) found that strategies asking students to identify similarities and differences led to an *average percentile gain of 45 points* in student achievement (p. 7).

One reason that comparison strategies yield such high levels of achievement is that humans are born *pairers* and *comparers*. Just think of all the pairings we make—Romeo and Juliet, sun and moon, peanut butter and jelly, and on and on. Although some of our peers in the humanities might not believe this, we math folks are also humans and love mathematical pairings. Just look at the sets of numbers we study—odd and even, positive and negative, rational and irrational, prime and composite . . . you get the picture. This tendency to see content in pairs deepens comprehension in at least four ways:

1. It enhances retention. Two ideas "joined at the hip" stay in our memories longer than ideas that are "loners." For example, by associating two related concepts—say, area and perimeter—we help both concepts stick around in our memories.

2. It lets us use what we already know to make sense of new information. For example, understanding fractions makes it much easier to understand decimals.

3. It spurs us to take a more analytical approach, to seek and find connections that might otherwise remain hidden.

4. It makes the abstract more concrete and the easily confused clearer. For example, we know that students often confuse the terms *expression* and *equation*. Asking students to compare examples of both, side by side, can significantly reduce that confusion.

The Compare and Contrast strategy releases the full power of comparative thinking by leading students through a four-phase learning process. First, students build their comprehension of the two items by describing each one separately using specific criteria. Second, they use a visual organizer to identify similarities and differences. Third, once the comparison is complete, students are asked to draw conclusions. For example, students might have to decide if the items are more alike or more different and explain why. Finally, students put their new learning to use by designing new problems, working on a group project, or some other meaningful synthesis task.

Planning Considerations

Determining Purpose and Content

Start with your purpose. Why are you asking students to use comparison? What benefits or mathematical insights will students gain from the comparison? Be prepared to answer these questions directly to your students: "We have learned how to rewrite a fraction as a percentage and to rewrite a fraction as a decimal. Let's compare two problems that use these processes to see when each might be especially useful." Why so much initial focus on explaining purpose to students? Because students are much more likely to commit to the lesson if they understand what they are doing and how it will help them.

As far as content selection goes, look for paired concepts, problems, and patterns that will enhance students' understanding. Positive and negative, rational and irrational, prime and composite, increasing and decreasing, greatest common factor and least common multiple, greater than and less than, proper and improper fractions, concave and convex, relation and function, inclusive and exclusive, metric system and English system, surface area and volume . . . the list goes on and on. You can also use Compare and Contrast to great effect by pairing problems or mathematical processes. For example, asking students to compare two different problems involving ratios will help students gain greater insight into the procedure and increase their ability to analyze and find the subtleties residing within the problems.

Planning for the Four Classroom Phases

In the *description phase,* students observe and describe each item separately. So, to plan for this phase, you'll need to ask, What sources of information will students use? Students may well need more than their memories to generate good descriptions of the items, expressions, or concepts. Will they use their textbooks, notebooks, or some other information sources to help them develop a complete description?

Next, focus on the criteria. Keep students' attention focused on the important points and ideas (e.g., for a comparison between triangular prism and rectangular prism, clear criteria could be number of sides of base, number of prism faces, number of prism vertices, and number of prism edges). In the beginning, you'll probably want to provide criteria to your own students. But as students get more comfortable using Compare and Contrast, you can work with them to generate criteria. Eventually, students should be able to develop criteria on their own.

In the *comparison phase,* students use a visual organizer to identify similarities and differences between the two items. Planning for this phase means selecting the organizer for the comparison. Several common comparative organizers are shown in Figure 2.6 on page 66.

During the *conclusion phase,* students discuss the relationship between the items and draw conclusions. So, what's involved in planning for this phase? Developing some thought-provoking discussion questions that will guide discussion and lead students to develop a conclusion:

* Are the items more alike or more different?
* How do we distinguish one from the other?
* What do you think is the most important difference?
* What generalizations can you make based on the similarities you found?
* What might be the causes or reasons behind some of the differences and similarities?

The *application phase* asks students to synthesize what they have learned and put it to use. Typically in planning for this phase, you'll design a synthesis task for students to complete. Synthesis tasks can be anything from a summary to a problem-solving task depending on your objectives.

Variations and Extensions

Comparative Analysis and Decision Making

A great tool for helping students use comparative analysis and mathematical reasoning to make good decisions is a Decision Making Matrix.

Side-by-Side Diagram

	Ruler	Protractor	Compass
What it measures			
Units of measurement used			
How to use it (procedure)			

Y Organizer

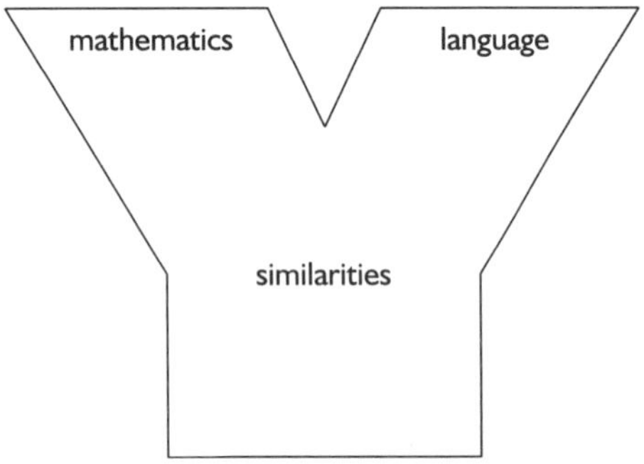

mathematics   language

similarities

Venn Diagram

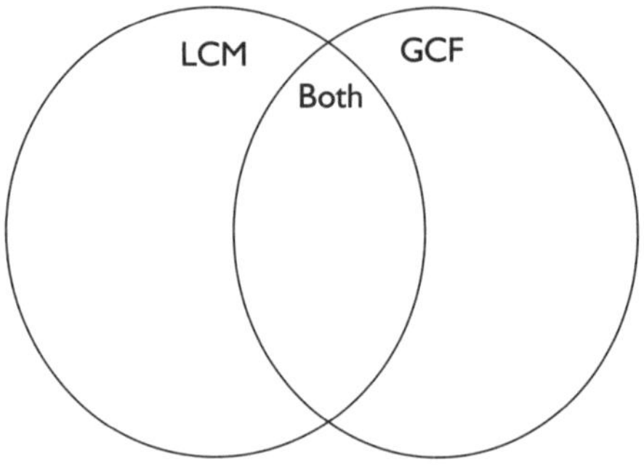

LCM   GCF

Both

Top Hat Organizer

Problem 1	Problem 2
If the two shorter sides of a right triangle are 6 and 8, find the longest side.	If the two longer sides of a right triangle are 12 and 13, find the shortest side.

Similarities

FIGURE 2.6 Compare and Contrast Organizers

Working with a Decision Making Matrix, students analyze three or more options (for example, Which of these three vacation destinations is best for me?) according to a list of attributes common to all of the options. Students then evaluate the options, numerically rank them using a one to three scale (3 is very important; 1 is not important), and determine how well each option meets or fulfills each criterion based on a zero to three scale (3 is completely; 0 is not at all).

Figure 2.7 shows how a teacher helped one of her students complete a Decision Making Matrix as a way to analyze the features and benefits of three different digital cameras.

Attributes	Importance 3 = Very Important 2 = Important 1 = Not Important	Brands of Digital Cameras		
		Canon	Kodak	Sony
		These brands of digital cameras meet my criteria: Completely (3); Considerably (2); Somewhat (1); Not at All (0)		
Price	3	3 • 2 = 6	3 • 3 = 9	3 • 1 = 3
Megapixels	3	3 • 1 = 3	3 • 1 = 3	3 • 3 = 9
Optical Zoom	2	2 • 3 = 6	2 • 2 = 4	2 • 2 = 4
Flash	1	1 • 3 = 3	1 • 0 = 0	1 • 2 = 2
Battery Life	2	2 • 2 = 4	2 • 1 = 2	2 • 2 = 4
Weight	1	1 • 2 = 2	1 • 0 = 0	1 • 3 = 3
Total Score		24	18	(25)

This is the best choice for me!

FIGURE 2.7 Student's Decision Making Matrix for Digital Cameras

Organizer B: Description Organizer

Math Problem/Concept:	Criteria for Comparison:	Math Problem/Concept:

Organizer C: Comparison Organizer

Math Problem/Concept:	Math Problem/Concept:

Similarities

Concept Attainment

Strategy Overview

So many essential concepts in mathematics are taught in the least memorable and most passive of ways: through textbook definitions or bald statements. To tell students, "A function is a mathematical relation in which each element of the domain is paired with exactly one element of the range," is to virtually guarantee that their interest will be low, that their understanding will be superficial, and their retention short. But, having students compare examples and nonexamples of functions in order to develop a set of critical attributes has an opposite effect: Learning becomes an active search, and comprehension grows in light of new discoveries.

The Concept Attainment strategy is based on the work of the great psychologist and educational theorist, Jerome Bruner (1960; 1973), and his research into how humans categorize information and develop conceptual understanding. What Bruner found is that no matter how many times a concept's definition is repeated, without an active process of testing and refining that concept, students will never get a firm grasp on this new information. They might very well be able to recite the glossary definition for a quadratic equation, but their understanding will have no analytical depth behind it. Their definition will not provide them with a clear way to determine the difference between a quadratic equation and a nonquadratic equation that can be expressed in quadratic form, for example. When it comes time for students to apply their understanding, they will likely flounder. Even worse, students will not have an adequate foundation on which to build future understanding—a situation that compounds itself with each new lesson and leaves the student further and further behind.

In response, Bruner discussed a teaching and learning process we call Concept Attainment. In using this strategy, the teacher selects a concept to be studied and presents examples and nonexamples—which have some but not all of the critical attributes—of the concept. Students must compare and contrast the examples and nonexamples, develop a working hypothesis that lists the critical attributes, test their hypothesis against further examples and nonexamples, and articulate the concept in their own words.

How to Use the Strategy

To implement the Concept Attainment strategy in your classroom, follow the steps below.

1. Select a concept with clear critical attributes (e.g., prime numbers, conic sections, linear equations) that you want students to understand deeply.

2. Provide students with examples that contain all of the critical attributes of the concept as well as nonexamples that contain some, but not all, of the attributes.

3. Ask students to identify what all the examples have in common and how the examples differ from the nonexamples. Students should generate an initial list of critical attributes of the concept.

4. Provide more examples and nonexamples for students to use in testing and refining their initial list of attributes.

5. As a whole class, review the examples and nonexamples, and generate a final set of critical attributes.

6. Ask students to apply their understanding of the concept by completing an activity.

The Strategy in Action

Kayla Mattine's students are learning about number theory. Today, she is using Concept Attainment to introduce her students to prime numbers.

Kayla begins by telling her students, "Today, we're going to learn about a new idea in number theory. I would like us to work together as a group to discover the patterns that will reveal this idea and describe it mathematically. Here's how I would like us to work: I'll give you positive examples of the idea, which we'll call *yes* ideas, and negative examples, which we'll call *no* ideas. I want you all to observe the examples carefully and really think about them. Let's see if we can use these examples to help us describe my idea."

Kayla divides the board into two narrow columns and one wide column. She labels the two narrow columns "Yes" and "No." She labels the remaining column "Description." Then, she lists the first few examples (Figure 2.8).

She waits, and then she asks the students to write down three ideas that occur to them as they study the examples. Bobby groans, "I know the answer already. Why do I need three?" His classmates respond with a chorus of agreement.

Kayla explains that she's not sure there's enough evidence yet and that they should try to get at least one other possibility in case they're wrong. After waiting a few moments, she asks Bobby to share his idea.

Yes	No	Description
3	4	
5	6	
7	8	

FIGURE 2.8 Kayla's First Examples

Bobby says, "Odd numbers. All of the examples are odd numbers." Kayla asks for a description, and records it in the description column: "All odd; even numbers are *no.*"

Yes	No	Description
3	4	All odd; even numbers are "no."
5	6	
7	8	

FIGURE 2.9 Description of First Examples

"Now," says Kayla, "here is another number, 9, which is a *no.*" The students are confused—and intrigued. Kayla asks, "So, what did you just learn?"

"Our idea is wrong," says Bobby. "If 9 is a *no,* and it is an odd number, then *yes* can't just be all odd numbers. Maybe some odd numbers belong, but not all of them. Why is 9 a *no?*"

"Good question, Bobby," says Kayla. "Let's look at the lists and see if we can figure out why 9 is a *no* and not a *yes.*"

As students propose ideas, Kayla writes them in the description column without passing judgment. If the students are in agreement that a previously suggested idea is not correct, she insists that they provide evidence from the list and then crosses it out, but she does not erase it. When student ideas falter, she offers additional examples.

"What about the number 2?" Kayla asks the students. "How many of you think it is a *yes?* How many of you think 2 is a *no?* The number 2 is a *yes.* Why?"

Kayla encourages her students to observe the characteristics of all the numbers in each column. She asks, "What do you know about these numbers?" She encourages her students to brainstorm ideas with their neighbors.

Finally, one of the students tentatively offers, "I don't think there is anything that can go into any of the *yes* numbers, but you can divide all of the *no* numbers." Kayla writes that description on the board, and then asks students to check the evidence.

Everyone agrees that the description is accurate until another student speaks up, "Wait. What about the number 1? Every number can be divided by 1."

Kayla suggests that her students list the *yes* and *no* numbers and write out their factors to check this idea. Excitement builds as students start to discover a pattern: All of the numbers from the *yes* column have exactly two factors, 1 and the number itself. The numbers from the *no* column have these factors plus other ones as well.

Kayla announces that the class has correctly identified the idea, and asks them to suggest a definition for the *yes* column. The agreed-upon definition reads, "Our idea is a number that can be divided by exactly two factors, 1 and itself." At this point, Kayla tells the class that these numbers are called *primes* and asks students to find five more primes between 15 and 50 for homework.

Why the Strategy Works

Too often, mathematical concepts are presented to students passively: The teacher writes information on the board or overhead, and, in turn, the students copy what's been written with very little thought. For students, this type of instruction results in only a superficial understanding of the concepts that won't be meaningful or lasting. Concept Attainment remedies this all-too-common scenario by having students identify the attributes of a mathematical concept through the critical analysis of *yes* and *no* examples.

The Concept Attainment strategy taps into the power that making predictions has on student learning, and is built off the research of Jerome Bruner (1960; 1973), who found that students need to actively test and refine new concepts before they can fully understand them. Bruner's work has been confirmed by a new generation of educational researchers studying the effectiveness of generating and testing hypotheses for improving student understanding and academic achievement (Linn & Eylon, 2006; Marzano, 2007; Marzano, Pickering, & Pollock, 2001; McClelland, 1994).

Planning Considerations

In designing a Concept Attainment activity, keep the following tips in mind:

1. The Concept Attainment strategy is most effective when introducing important and distinguishable mathematical concepts. What distinguishes key mathematical concepts from trivial ones that are not so important? Key concepts are ones that are central to their respective strands and serve as critical tools for problem solving. Examples of important mathematical concepts include *perfect squares, prime numbers, perfect trinomials, the Pythagorean theorem,* and *functions.*

2. Examples in the Concept Attainment activity need to exclusively represent the featured concept. Students will focus on the examples to uncover the mathematical concept they are looking for. If a teacher is not careful, it is possible to create a list of examples that is misleading to students. For example, think about the concept "multiples of four" in relation to the numbers 8, 16, 24, and 40. While it's true that all the examples are multiples of four, they all happen to be multiples of eight also. A better set of examples would be 4, 16, 24, and 28. The inclusion of *4* and *28* in the examples set rules out "multiples of eight" as the represented concept.

3. Nonexamples in the Concept Attainment activity need to be ones that help students eliminate likely but wrong concepts. They can also partially fit the criteria of the examples. For the examples 4, 16, 24, and 28, representing multiples of four, a good set of nonexamples might be 7, 6, 9, and 22. Initially, when 4 and 7 are revealed, students might guess even versus odd. Next, when 16 and 6 are revealed, students would know that the featured concept is not even numbers because the number 6 appears in the nonexamples. After eliminating even numbers and perfect squares, students will likely be poised to examine and discover the concept multiples of four.

4. During the Concept Attainment process, provide time for students to analyze the data, develop their thoughts, process similarities and differences, and form conclusions. The critical thinking and communication components of the Concept Attainment activity are the key elements that produce understanding and retention. Be sure to allow time for these processes to take place. Hurrying students along or giving in to the temptation to just tell the students the answer will only undercut the academic benefit of the strategy.

Variations and Extensions

Concept Identification

A great variation on the Concept Attainment strategy is Concept Identification. The Concept Identification strategy is a simplified version of Concept Attainment. Rather than teaching new concepts, Concept Identification helps students practice skills and review mathematical concepts. Through this strategy, teachers can make practice far more fun and interesting than simply assigning problems and listening to student groans: Practice becomes a search for a mystery answer or a minipuzzle to be solved. The teacher presents students with two sets of practice problems. One set of problems, labeled *yes*, has solutions that conform to a specific mathematical concept or criteria while the other, labeled *no*, does not. The students are challenged to work with a learning partner to solve both sets of problems. Once both sets of problems have been solved and correct answers have been confirmed, students then must analyze the solutions of the *yes* problems to identify the concept represented by those solutions. The solutions of the *no* problems can be used to verify or rule out particular concepts and assist students in their thinking.

Below is a simple sample of a Concept Identification challenge set.

Yes: $20 - 5 + 35 - 2$ *No:* $20 - 6 + 3$
$\quad\quad 1 - 8 + 3 + 4$ $15 - 20 + 20 - 8$
$\quad\quad 10 + 10 - -4$ $-10 + 20 - 1$
$\quad\quad 12 - 2 - 2$ $12 - 2 + 1$
$\quad\quad -5 + 8 + 12$ $-5 + 58 - 3$

The answers to the problems in the *yes* set are 48, 0, 24, 8, and 15. The answers to the problems in the *no* set are 17, 7, 9, 11, and 50. The identified concept is *numbers that are one less than perfect squares.* The Concept Identification activity is not only fun for students but can also bring attention to two concepts instead of one. In this case, the two concepts are *combining integers* and *perfect squares.*

Knowledge Cards

Knowledge Cards are a great way for students to process and retain concepts they've developed through Concept Attainment. They also make for a great synthesis activity. To develop a knowledge card for each concept, students create a memorable icon on one side of the card and compose a descriptive summary on the other side. Figure 2.10 shows one student's Knowledge Cards for *translation* and *reflection*.

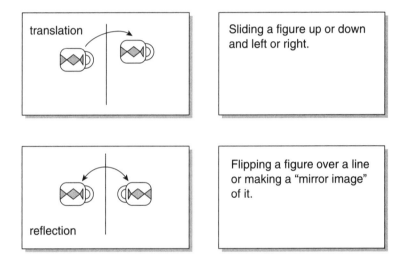

FIGURE 2.10 Sample Knowledge Cards

Source: Silver, H. F., Brunsting, J. R., & Walsh, T. (2008). *Math Tools, Grades 3–12: 64 Ways to Differentiate Instruction and Increase Student Engagement.* (p. 21).

Math Busters: Developing a Mathematical Argument

Strategy Overview

MythBusters (Rees et al., 2003–present) is a cable television show that puts popular myths to the test by asking the question, "Can that actually be true?" Can people really walk on hot coals without burning their feet? Is that story about Pop Rocks and soda causing a boy's stomach to explode really plausible? If you drop a penny from a skyscraper, can it really generate enough force to kill someone? *MythBusters* uses tools of science to separate the truth from urban legend.

In Math Busters, students use the tools of mathematics to put mathematical claims to the test. Mathematical claims are everywhere, and many of them are designed to influence students' beliefs. Advertisers, politicians, and the media in general rely on numbers and statistics to make their cases more persuasive. Very often, all that is needed to test these claims is a clear and mathematically sound procedure for assembling and analyzing facts. Math Busters teaches students this procedure as a series of six steps:

1. Clearly identify the claim

2. Develop a hypothesis of your initial belief or disbelief in the claim

3. Collect, organize, and display relevant data

4. Perform and display appropriate calculations

5. Draw a logical conclusion

6. Communicate your findings

Students can apply this procedure to a wide range of mathematical claims, from advertisements, to claims based on the graphical and numerical data in their textbooks, to teacher-designed claims (e.g., *the average American's heart beats over three billion times in his or her lifetime*), and even to students' own preconceptions and opinions, which often revolve around mathematical assumptions (for example, you might survey the class's beliefs about how many hours the average cell phone user spends texting and then use it to form a claim).

How to Use the Strategy

The main purpose behind Math Busters is to teach students how to use mathematical thinking to analyze claims and draw sound conclusions.

Once you have provided (or worked with students to develop) a scenario involving a mathematical claim, lead them through the six steps in the Math Busters procedure:

1. Clearly identify the claim. Make sure students take the time to isolate the claim and to state it in their own words.

2. Develop a hypothesis. Does the claim pass the students' initial "smell test"? Do they believe it or reject it? Students should develop a working hypothesis about the truth of the claim before they begin analyzing it.

3. Collect, organize, and display relevant data. Once students have a hypothesis, they can begin to develop and execute a plan for proving it or disproving it. Depending on the complexity of the research, you may choose to work with students to help them decide what kinds of information they need to collect to test the claim. As students become more comfortable with the process, they can make these decisions with greater independence.

4. Perform and display appropriate calculations. What mathematical operations do students need to perform to prove or disprove the claim? Be sure that students clearly show their work, as they will need it to support their conclusions.

5. Draw a logical conclusion. Does the claim hold up? Was their initial hypothesis correct, or does it need revision?

6. Communicate their findings. Ask students to share what they learned. Engage the class in a discussion not only about the claim, but also about their own mathematical thinking during the process.

You should make the steps in this procedure explicit to students. That way, you can shift responsibility for applying the steps to them. Explain to students that these steps are more than the components in a strategy: They represent a powerful process that will help them become better thinkers and consumers.

The Strategy in Action

Here we look at the steps in the Math Busters strategy and model how a student might work her way through these steps. So, let's imagine that students are presented with the following scenario:

A conservation group implemented a campaign to encourage people to save water. In their literature they asked people to not leave the water running in the bathroom sink while brushing their teeth. They argued that over a billion gallons of water could be saved in the United States annually if people just turned the water off while brushing their teeth.

Claim: The student would begin by identifying the claim and stating it in her own words, like this: Over one billion gallons of water can be saved each year in the United States if people turn off their faucets while brushing their teeth.

Hypothesis: Upon discussion with a learning partner, the student might choose to disagree with the claim.

Gathering Data: Students might plan to determine the truth of the claim by performing an experiment at home in which they let the water run into a measured container while brushing their teeth. They might ask other family members to participate in the experiment.

After approximating the amount of water lost to running water, they would bring their data to school and share it with their partner. Partners might gather necessary additional data by (a) polling classmates and family members to determine how often people brush their teeth and (b) checking the U.S. population given on the national census website. Other students might take their data gathering a step further by polling to determine how many people already turn the water off while brushing their teeth and then establishing a rough percentage of "water runners."

Calculation: Students might multiply the U.S. population (or estimate a nationwide percentage of "water runners" based on their chosen method of gathering data) by the number of times people brush their teeth in a day, times the average amount of water lost while brushing teeth. Subtractions from the population census number might be made for infants and elderly people without teeth.

Conclusion: Students would then compare their calculated water-conservation estimate with the number in the claim and draw a conclusion as to whether the claim is plausible or implausible.

Communication: Students communicate their findings to the class and discuss variations in their methods and their findings.

Math Buster problem-solving approaches will often vary significantly. In addressing claims, students may find missing information or hidden questions, which, in turn, cause them to raise questions of their own. Because of the different choices students make and the variety of thinking they apply, Math Buster problems provide rich, thought-provoking learning activities that spur serious—and engaging—discussions. Of course, not all Math Busters need to come from the media or involve outside research. Thoughtful Math Buster activities can be designed by modifying textbook problems, as shown in the two examples that follow.

Directions: Each problem below describes a real-world problem-solving situation that includes a startling claim. Work with a learning partner and follow the prescribed six Math Buster steps to produce a thorough argument that supports or refutes the claim. Be sure to include mathematical hypotheses, experiments, data, calculations, and summaries that justify your solution.

Problem 1: On the first day of school, Tiffany Forester asked her fourth-grade students to share what they had done over their summer vacations. A student named William said he spent most of his time riding his bicycle. In fact, William claimed that *he rode his bike so much over the summer that he traveled a sum total of miles greater than the distance from their school in Savannah, Georgia, to San Francisco, California.*

Support or refute William's claim.

Problem 2: Toby loved to play with tin foil. He particularly enjoyed folding and creasing it. One day, while folding and creasing his tin foil, he made the following claim: *If I had a super large sheet of tin foil that was just one millimeter thick and folded it in half 100 times, the measure of the thickness of the folded stack would be greater than the distance of 100 round trips between the Earth and the sun.*

Support or refute Toby's claim.

Why the Strategy Works

In *The Art and Science of Teaching*, Robert Marzano (2007) poses ten distinct questions that instructional research compels all teachers to ask. The reason teachers need to ask these questions when they design and deliver instruction is that each question, when answered well, leads to dramatic increases in student achievement. In short, by compiling the findings from decades worth of research on what works best in the classroom, Marzano has identified the ten most effective ways to promote high levels of achievement, and he articulated each in the form of a simple question. Of Marzano's ten questions, Math Busters responds directly to two: *What will I do to engage students?* and *What will I do to help students generate and test hypotheses about new knowledge?*

Let's start with engagement. How is Math Busters engaging for students? Well, for one thing, Math Busters is decidedly not passive math. Math Busters is a direct invitation into the content. Students are encouraged to let their inner skeptics out and to challenge conventional thinking. To further increase student engagement, teachers can take a cue from Adam Savage and Jamie Hyneman, the hosts of the show *MythBusters,* from which this strategy draws its name. Adam and Jamie pursue their investigations with zeal and wonder; they take joy in pitting their minds against popular assumptions and common wisdom. Math Busters activities can and should be driven by the same spirit of inquiry and investigation.

Next, we turn our attention to Marzano's question about generating and testing hypotheses, which is the core thinking process that animates Math Busters. Since the famous psychologist and educational pioneer Jerome Bruner (1960) highlighted the critical roles that prediction and confirmation play in the human learning process, a large number of research studies have shown that teaching students how to generate and test hypotheses is one of the best ways to sharpen students' thinking skills and raise their test scores. In fact, Marzano's research suggests that students who are taught the generating-and-testing-hypotheses process perform at an achievement level that's roughly 20 percentile points higher than students in classrooms where the process goes untaught.

Planning Considerations

Creating a Math Busters application requires the teacher to pay close attention to three interrelated activity design elements: content (or claim), information sources, and task management.

Paying Attention to Content (Claim)

The content of a Math Busters activity is essentially wrapped up in its focused claim and related information and facts. Many teachers of mathematics begin planning with specific content in mind. Once selected, the content (e.g., slope-intercept form) can be readily located in textbooks and any related information and facts selected (definition of slope-intercept form, slope meaning and value, y-intercept, etc.). Once you've got your information, a claim can easily be developed (e.g., *every line can be written in the form $y = mx + b$*). Make sure you determine whether the claim is true or false. (The claim above is false.)

On the other hand, claims often will appear first. We are bombarded daily with sales promises and intriguing TV or radio claims. Discerning listeners search for personal prior knowledge or use their intuition to evaluate these claims. In such scenarios, the claims come before the information, and sound something like this: *Dogs and cats consume almost $7 billion worth of pet food a year.*

Using real-world claims and encouraging students to develop a healthy skepticism along with an analytical approach to "claim-busting" is worthy of class time and encouraged by NCTM Standards (2000).

Paying Attention to Information Sources

You also need to know what information or facts will be required to test a particular claim. Sometimes, all the necessary information is provided within the Math Buster. Other times, students will need to seek information from sources that are available within their classroom or, for more involved inquiries, perhaps available only outside the classroom. What resources are needed and where students need to go to secure the information will impact the scope of the assignment. Let's look at three options for how information might be provided to students as they evaluate this claim: *There is a linear relationship between the number of rooms in a house and the total number of electrical outlets in a house.*

- All of the information needed to support or refute the Math Buster claim is included: For three homes, the set of ordered pairs {(5,16), (6,20), (8,28)} relates the total number of rooms in a house and the total number of electrical outlets in each house. A linear relationship exists between the two variables x and y; if $y = mx + b$ for all x, y is in the set.
- Some of the information is not provided but is available in textbooks or other classroom resources: The set of ordered pairs {(4,20), (6,24), (7,28)} relates the total number of rooms in a house and the total number of electrical outlets, respectively.
- Students receive only the claim and have to conduct research to fill in the gaps of information.

Paying Attention to Task Management

Finally, Math Buster activities must include adequate time for student thought, discussion, and work. The content and information decisions will determine the complexity of the task. The more complex the task, the more time will be needed, and the more you might consider having students work in partnerships or teams.

Variations and Extensions

Fun Facts

Andrew Barnes uses a variation on the Math Busters strategy by creating a number of data-rich information statements. Each statement, called a Fun Fact, cites data but does not include any claim. One of Andrew's Fun Facts is reprinted below:

Fun Fact: Over 80,000 eggs are scrambled, fried, poached, and hard-boiled each week by the cooks of the city's restaurants. These same restaurants serve nearly 7,000 customers each day of the week. A hen requires 24 to 26 hours to produce a single egg and thirty minutes later, it starts all over again. The world population of chickens is approximately equal to the world's population of people.

Andrew organizes students into teams and gives each team a single Fun Fact statement. No two teams receive the same Fun Fact statement.

Andrew then gives teams of students 12 minutes to create a verifiable Math Buster claim based on their Fun Facts. Andrew encourages teams to design their claims so that they are likely to fool their classmates. Below is one team's claim based on the Fun Facts above.

Claim for Fun Fact: The egg suppliers for the city's restaurants will need between 10,000 to 12,000 hens to meet the demand for eggs each week.

Along with their created claim, each team provides a written solution that clearly supports or refutes the claim.

At the end of the allotted time, Andrew collects the student-generated claims along with the distributed Fun Facts statements. Using a projector, he displays each Fun Fact and associated claim one by one. Student teams have one minute to read each Fun Fact and claim, discuss their hypotheses, and record their initial ideas.

Andrew surveys the class and tallies the number of students who believe that the claim is true or false.

Fun Facts statements, now with an associated claim, are then randomly redistributed to each student team, with no team receiving its original Fun Facts statement. Each team gets 10 minutes to apply the Math Buster steps to their claim and determine its validity.

After a round of discussion, Andrew has each team grade their initial true-false hunches and, as a class, determine which Math Buster claim fooled the most students.

3

Self-Expressive
Strategies

OVERVIEW

Self-Expressive strategies help students *visualize* mathematics and *think flexibly* and *creatively* to solve *nonroutine problems.*

Self-Expressive math students . . .

- *Want to* use their imagination to explore mathematical ideas.
- *Like math problems that* are nonroutine, project-like in nature, and that allow them to think outside the box.
- *Approach problem solving* by visualizing the problem, generating possible solutions, and exploring among the alternatives.
- *Experience difficulty when* mathematics instruction is focused on drill-and-practice and rote problem solving.
- *Want a math teacher who* invites imagination and creative problem solving into the mathematics classroom.

The four Self-Expressive strategies in this chapter can help you meet these NCTM Process Standards.

Strategy	NCTM Process Standards*				
	Problem Solving	Reasoning and Proof	Communication	Connections	Representation
Metaphorical Expression [p. 85] Students use metaphors, such as direct analogies, personal analogies, and compressed conflicts, to explore mathematical concepts by making the strange familiar or the familiar strange.			✓	✓	✓
3-D Viewer [p. 92] Students represent mathematical concepts and solve problems using variables or symbols, graphs, and tables of data.	✓	✓	✓	✓	✓
Modeling and Experimentation [p. 99] Through teacher modeling and in-class experimentation, students learn how to accurately represent, manipulate, and compute the symbols and numbers that are representations of abstract mathematical ideas.	✓			✓	✓
Inductive Learning [p. 113] Students group and label a set of terms, equations, numbers, or other data, then make and test hypotheses about their classifications.		✓	✓	✓	

FIGURE 3.0   Correlation of Self-Expressive Strategies to NCTM Process Standards

*For more information on the National Council of Teachers of Mathematics (NCTM) Process Standards, please consult their *Principles and Standards for School Mathematics* (2000), or visit their website at www.nctm.org.

Metaphorical Expression

Strategy Overview

How is mathematics like a language? How is a number line like an elevator? How is solving an equation like digestion? How is an equation like a balance scale? As an instructional strategy, Metaphorical Expression poses these kinds of comparisons, placing two seemingly unrelated concepts side by side, inviting imagination into mathematics and mathematical thinking.

Metaphorical Expression challenges students to think deeply about a particular mathematical concept by exploring, discovering, and communicating analogous relationships between that concept and a topic or object that, at its surface, is nothing like the concept under investigation. These seemingly far-fetched connections force students' minds into activity; the further they stretch, the deeper the conceptual understanding becomes, and the stronger their memories grow.

How to Use the Strategy

The true power of Metaphorical Expression lies in its ability to stimulate and set free student thought and expression. When presenting and discussing Metaphorical Expression activities, teachers should be very careful to not inadvertently promote a mindset of a single correct answer. Indeed, teachers may well need to model such freedom of thought in order to release students from the common misconception that mathematics questions and problems have one right answer. Of course, the fact that there are many possible responses does not mean that every response is as good as every other. The real test of an idea is in how well the student can explain the connection.

Metaphorical Expression can be used to review and process already-taught concepts or to introduce new ones. Here's how each lesson type (processing or introducing) works.

- As a review and processing technique, Metaphorical Expression encourages students to tap into prior knowledge and look for meaningful connections. For example, after introducing and practicing a set of problem-solving steps, Melanie Majors asked her middle school students to compare problem solving with the process of hiking up a mountain. Her students found the following parallels:
- First, prepare for the challenge by gathering the problem facts or mountain's characteristics. Some facts may be irrelevant.
  - Identify the question to be answered or final destination
  - Create and label a diagram, or find a good map

- Develop a plan of attack, but know that you may have to make detours
- Both are work but may be fun, especially if we work with others.
- Both may be seen as adventures.

• When using Metaphorical Expression to introduce new concepts, the idea is to suggest characteristics of not-yet-presented material. These characteristics or links will then be "looked for" as the new material is presented. For example, Joel Krebs introduced right triangle ratios ("trig" ratios) by telling his geometry class that, "A trigonometric ratio is like a bridge." His students began the unit by thinking about and listing bridge characteristics (e.g., fixed structures that connect two pieces of land, travelers can go either way on them, different bridges connect different things, they provide helpful shortcuts, and they span something difficult to cross). Students speculated what might be true of these new things called trigonometric ratios. A simple bridge was drawn on poster board and named the "Trig Ratio Bridge" (Figure 3.1). As the unit was taught, the Trig Ratio Bridge was used as an organizer to identify the common characteristics.

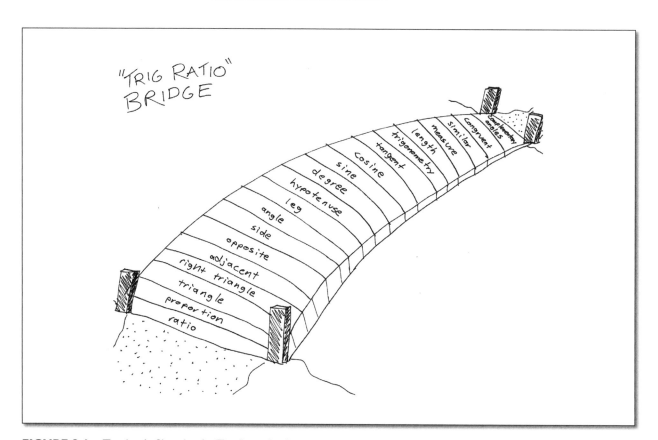

FIGURE 3.1 Teacher's Sketch of a Trig Ratio Bridge

When using any Metaphorical Expression activity, students should be encouraged to

1. Be creative and flexible in their thinking;

2. Make sure they understand the mathematics involved, so they can make quality connections (to this end, you may want to help "spill the pickles" by reviewing or letting students review the mathematical concept before engaging in metaphorical thinking);

3. Be comprehensive in their search for relationships; and

4. Provide clear explanations of the relationships they cite.

The Strategy in Action

Arturo Franklin is using Metaphorical Expression to help his students process and internalize the relationships among the various quadrilaterals they have been studying. After noting that the form of his unit organizer looked very much like the structure of a genealogy family tree, he developed the metaphorical question, How is the set of quadrilaterals like a family tree?

Before posing that question to the class, Arturo models metaphorical thinking with a purely nonmathematical metaphorical question, "How is life like a book?" As he suspects, his students had no difficulty finding parallels. After only a few minutes of discussion, Arturo explains, "Just as a metaphor helped us find interesting connections between life and a book, metaphors can help us understand mathematical concepts, processes, or terms, like *quadrilateral.*"

Arturo then poses his strategic question, "How is the set of quadrilaterals like a family tree?" Before allowing students to answer the question, he leads a whole-class review and discussion session in

FIGURE 3.2 Family Tree

which the class identifies the complete set of quadrilaterals—squares, rectangles, trapezoids, parallelograms, rhombuses, isosceles trapezoids, and kites. During the discussion, Arturo also shows the class a family tree (Figure 3.2) and explains how it shows the relationships between extended family members.

Arturo divides the class into small groups and sets them loose brainstorming answers to the question How is the set of quadrilaterals like a family tree? Later, as students share their comparisons, Arturo keeps track of students' responses on the board.

The set of quadrilaterals is like a family tree because

- All its members are related through the definition of a quadrilateral (e.g., four-sided polygon).
- As in a real family tree, all quadrilaterals have names (rhombus, etc.).
- In families, inheritance is passed to offspring; quadrilaterals also inherit the properties of their "parent" shapes.
- While each family member may inherit characteristics of parents, each one has something special about itself.
- In the real world, one's family is small compared to the entire population. Similarly, the quadrilateral family is small compared to the entire "population" of polygons.
- There seems to be at least one black sheep in every family, and quadrilaterals have the kite!

After all of the groups share their observations, Arturo gives them a synthesis task. Students are free to select from one of these three tasks:

1. Write an interesting short story about a quadrilateral family in which you describe what each family member inherits and from whom.

2. Create a new (improved?) metaphor for the set of quadrilaterals. "How is the set of quadrilaterals like _____?" Provide at least four reasons that support the new metaphor.

3. Write an explanation of how metaphors can be helpful in understanding mathematical concepts.

In another classroom, Michele Tu wants her students to appreciate the technology and functionality of their calculators. So, she lets students create their own comparison for their calculators by posing an incomplete simile: "Using a calculator in mathematics is like _____."

Here is one student's response:

Using a calculator in mathematics is like *playing an instrument* because

- Instruments and calculators can manipulate notes or numbers one at a time.
- Instrument keys (strings) have specific functions like the keys of a calculator.
- A combination of calculator keys pressed simultaneously alters the result just as combinations of instrument keys (strings) alter the sound.
- Wrong notes played are mistakes like pressing the wrong keys on a calculator.
- Playing a musical score requires proper technique just like following the order of operations for a mathematical expression.
- Practice helps you get better at using both.
- Calculators and instruments both help their users express what's in their minds.

Why the Strategy Works

Simplicity is part of the beauty and power of Metaphorical Expression. With just a few words, a metaphor opens up a world of ideas for exploration. What's more, metaphorical thinking is one of the most effective ways to improve comprehension and raise achievement. For example:

- Metaphorical Expression activities promote creative and divergent thinking—two forms of higher-level thinking proven to increase conceptual understanding (Cole & McLeod, 1999; Chen, 1999).
- Marzano, Pickering, and Pollock's (2001) research into effective instructional strategies shows that strategies that ask students to search for similarities and differences lead to greater gains in student-achievement levels than any other type of strategy.
- The Metaphorical Expression strategy promotes holistic understanding of concepts because it draws on both sides of the brain, the analytical reasoning side and the creative, imaginative side.
- Metaphors appeal to creative students who often feel left out or stifled by traditional mathematics instruction.

Planning Considerations

In designing and using a Metaphorical Expression, you may find the following tips helpful.

1. Plan to introduce metaphorical thinking to students. Model the metaphorical-thinking process for students by comparing a mathematics concept with a nonmathematical one. Have fun with it! "How is mathematics like a language?" is a good way to begin, but here are a few more of an endless number of possibilities:

- How is simplifying an expression like organizing the stuff in a junk drawer?

- How is solving a word problem like a United Nations translator?
- How is a direct equation like a sales tax?
- How is an indirect equation like the light from a reading lamp?
- How is a proportion like a four-legged table?
- How is the absolute value function like a light switch?

2. Decide if your purpose is to deepen processing of already-learned material or to introduce a new concept. You can use metaphors to help students gain new insights and deeper understanding of mathematical concepts they are already familiar with, or you can use metaphors to help students develop a strong grip on new content by introducing a new mathematical idea metaphorically. If students are unfamiliar with the mathematical concept, you'll need to spend some time giving them a basic introduction so they can develop a meaningful metaphorical comparison.

3. Select your mathematical concept and a nonmathematical item or object for comparison. Since mathematics correlates so well with the real world, students can be challenged to discover an analogous relationship between any two topics. If the purpose of the instructional activity is to improve students' understanding of mathematics, the real-world topic should be one that is well known and understood by the students. For example, the problem "show how radian measure of angles and the unit circle is like the distance a wheel of a bicycle travels" is more effective than "show how radian measure is like a stochastic process." Most students know next to nothing about stochastic processes and, therefore, would not be able to make rich connections. No matter what topic or object you choose, it is always a good idea to review it before asking students to use it on their own. To challenge students' creative thinking process even further, you may allow students to choose (rather than providing them with) the item or analog they would like to compare to the given mathematics concept.

4. Decide whether students will work independently, in groups, or both. Whatever you choose, allow students to think on their own and write down a few of their own thoughts before having them work with partners or in a small group.

5. Plan sufficient time for students to experience the activity without undue pressure. Plan time for sharing and explanations as well. Metaphors often lead to robust discussions in the classroom. Leave yourself enough time to let those discussions flourish.

6. Decide how students will synthesize their learning. Metaphorical Expression lessons lend themselves to all kinds of synthesis tasks. You can ask students to

- Create a new metaphor;
- Write a short story or other creative writing piece that features their metaphor; or
- Write an explanation of how metaphors enhance mathematical understanding.

Variations and Extensions

Metaphorical Duels

Metaphorical Duels pit two nonmathematical ideas against each other and ask students to choose and defend the idea that makes for the better comparison. For example, in place of asking, "How is a fraction like a piece of pizza?" you might ask, "Is a fraction more like a piece of pizza or *more like* a classroom filled with only blue-eyed students?"

Two nonmathematical choices provide additional comparison and relationship possibilities. This proves especially helpful with mathematics topics not yet fully understood by students.

3-D Viewer (Algebraic, Graphic, Numeric)

Strategy Overview

An old trend in moviemaking is new again as some of the biggest releases in Hollywood are being shown in 3-D. Three-dimensional movies create an experience that leaves moviegoers talking about what they've seen, heard, and felt. "The characters jumped right out of the big screen!" "The river seemed to cascade right down the aisles." "The cannon ball just missed our heads!" These movies are often more memorable because the additional "dimensions" enhance the experience. The same is true of art and architecture. After all, the best way to experience a Rodin sculpture or a Frank Lloyd Wright building is to explore the object from many angles in order to more fully appreciate its dimensionality. In a similar way, we can enhance our students' appreciation for and understanding of mathematical concepts by challenging them to explore mathematics from different perspectives.

The 3-D Viewer strategy builds students' representational fluency by asking them to analyze concepts using three mathematical perspectives or "dimensions": algebraic symbolism, graphic representation, and numeric data. 3-D Viewer then requires students to communicate their learning through all three dimensions, providing the teacher and student with valuable insight into the depth of student understanding.

For example, we can be sure that a learner understands deeply the quadratic's basic parent function if that student can see the concept in 3-D by

1. Identifying its algebraic forms, $y = x^2$ or $f(x) = x^2$ (algebraic dimension).

2. Visualizing its graphic form, parabola with vertex at the origin (graphic dimension; see Figure 3.3).

3. Recognizing its telltale squared numeric data in ordered-pair form (numeric dimension), {(-3,9), (-2,4), (-1,1), (0,0), (1,1), (2,4), (3,9)}, or tabular form (see Figure 3.4).

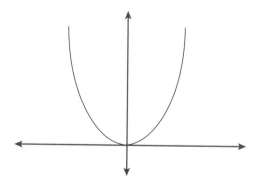

FIGURE 3.3   Graph of $y = x^2$

x	y
−3	9
−2	4
−1	1
0	0
1	1
2	4
3	9

FIGURE 3.4 Table of Data

Each perspective—algebraic, graphic, and numeric—affords a distinct representation of the basic quadratic. Yet, each viewpoint complements and enhances the other two. The algebraic is a shorthand perspective that empowers modeling, generates function values, and sets the stage for transformations; the graphic perspective enables visual "sight" of the function's elegant symmetry and behavior; the numeric perspective displays discrete x and y values generated by the algebraic form, highlighting individual solutions, the stuff graphs are made of, and the symmetry in ordered pairs or tables of values.

How to Use the Strategy

1. Introduce and model the 3-D Viewer process by showing students how they might represent a well-known math concept or problem algebraically, graphically, and numerically.

2. Introduce the mathematical concept, problem, or idea that students will by studying.

3. Have students work through the activity using all three approaches.

4. After each approach, allow students time to review their work and make notes.

5. Engage students in a whole-class discussion. Encourage students to compare the different representations, explain which approaches worked best for them, and draw conclusions about the concept under investigation.

6. To help students retain and apply what they've learned, you may ask them to complete a synthesis task that requires them to draw all three approaches.

The Strategy in Action

To ensure that his pre-algebra students understand the concept of *direct variation*, Howard Asher is using the 3-D Viewer strategy.

After thinking about direct variation from the algebraic, graphic, and numeric perspectives, Howard creates three questions, one of each 3-D type, develops a three-column organizer that could be used for side-by-side comparison, and composes several reflective questions for his students. He also decides that students would, at various times, work individually, as partners, and as a whole class.

He begins the direct variation lesson with the numeric perspective by presenting five sets of tabular data (see Figure 3.5). He tells the class that four of the tables represented examples of the new topic, direct variation, but one of the sets does not. He asks his students to study the data tables and share whatever observations they could make.

A		B		C		D		E	
x	y	x	y	x	y	x	y	x	y
−1	−3	3	6	1	0.5	0	0	1	1
0	0	2	4	1.5	0.75	0.2	20	2	0.5
1	3	0	0	3	1.5	0.4	40	4	0.25
2	6	1	2	3.5	1.75	0.8	80	10	0.1
3	9	−1	−2	2.5	1.25	0.9	90	100	0.01
4	13	−2	−4	2	1	1	10	1000	0.001

FIGURE 3.5   Five Tables of Data for a 3-D Viewer Lesson

After several minutes of study, one of his students, Rachel, says that she found a pattern in just three tables. Rachel explains that after reordering the ordered pairs in Tables B and C so x-values were in increasing order, she observed that in Tables A, B, and D, *as x-values increased, so did the y-values;* while in Tables C and E, *the y-values decreased.* Another student notes that the only thing that the four Tables A, B, C, and D have in common is that each contains at least one negative value of *y.* None of the students are confident that he or she could identify a meaningful characteristic that exactly four tables share.

After other students share their observations, Howard suggests that they look at the data from a graphic standpoint. He distributes graph paper and asks students to work with a learning partner and make separate graphs, one for each numeric table. Once all five graphs are made, the students discuss what, if anything, the graphs helped them see.

Each pair of students graph the data sets, and many students observe that the points in Tables A, B, C, and D form straight lines, while the data set E definitely does not form a line.

Howard confirms student observations about Tables A through D and says, "That when data behaves in this way, we say this is a direct variation and that 'y varies directly with x.'" He challenges his students to find an algebraic equation for Tables A, B, C, and D, and, if possible, for Table E.

Howard leads a class discussion to generate the general direct variation formula, $y = kx$. To help students synthesize their learning, Howard distributes a simple three-column 3-D Viewer organizer to each student.

Howard challenges each student to create a new direct variation (e.g., $y = 3x$), write its algebraic form under the first heading, generate a numeric

Algebraic	Numeric	Graphic

FIGURE 3.6 3-D Viewer Organizer

table for some of its data in column two, and draw its graph in the last column (Figure 3.6). At the bottom of each column, students are asked to complete the sentence, "If I only had this column's viewpoint, then I would describe direct variation as _____."

Another teacher, Richard Knoble, routinely uses 3-D Viewer in his algebra classes. Richard designs his 3-D Viewer lessons so that they are especially student centered (rather than teacher directed). For example:

1. After planning a review of the systems of linear equations, Richard challenged his students to explain what a solution to a system "is" algebraically, graphically, and numerically.

2. Students work in partner teams using 3-D Viewer to develop class definitions of all algebraic parent functions: constant, linear, quadratic, step, sign, and so on, with algebraic, graphic, and numeric perspectives.

3. Small groups of students are assigned one of the following problems and work collaboratively. Each problem is to be solved in three ways using 3-D Viewer:
   a. $y = -2x^2 + 7x$
   b. $y = -x^2 + 3x - 6$
   c. $y = -x^2 + 6x - 9$

4. Richard poses questions like these during his units: Find the maximum value of the quadratic function, algebraically, graphically and numerically. Explain which was the easiest. Which was the most difficult?

Why the Strategy Works

One relatively new development in mathematical research is the concept known as *representational fluency*. According to Zbiek, Heid, Blume, and Dick (2007), representational fluency involves three abilities:

1. The ability to translate mathematical ideas and meanings across different representations;

2. The ability to draw meaning about a mathematical concept from multiple representations of the concept; and

3. The ability to make generalizations using the information from different representations.

It should come as little surprise that students with a high degree of representational fluency achieve higher levels of success in mathematics classrooms than their less-fluent peers. Representations concretize the abstract concepts that make up much of the mathematics curriculum; therefore, students who have more ways at their disposal to concretize their learning—to cut through the abstraction—get a better handle on the content. Indeed, research shows that students who are able to represent mathematical ideas using multiple representations demonstrate deeper understanding (Hall, Kibler, Wenger, & Truxaw, 1989) and greater problem-solving capacity (Koedinger & Tabachneck, 1994). Koedinger and Tabachneck's study also suggests that representational fluency leads to long-term retention of mathematical learning, as representationally fluent students proved far superior in solving standard word problems years after they had learned the procedures for solving them. This finding correlates squarely with the more general research of Paivio (1990) whose dual-coding theory posits that different ways of representing information get stored in different parts of the brain, leading to increased memory and recall.

Few strategies place as much of a premium on representational fluency as 3-D Viewer. It asks students to explore and communicate regularly about concepts through three distinct "dimensions" or ways of representing mathematics: algebraic, graphic, and numeric.

Of course, technology can be a tremendous enhancement to a 3-D Viewer lesson. Handheld graphing calculators and computers can display, side by side, an algebraic equation, a table of solution points, and a graphic. Further, these three representations can be dynamically interactive so that a change made in the algebraic equation instantly generates new data and a new graph.

Planning Considerations

Developing a basic 3-D Viewer lesson or activity involves these steps:

1. Select an important mathematics concept or topic that students need to deeply understand—for example, *function;* specific function types such as *step function* or *absolute value function, slope, Pythagorean theorem, inverse*

variation, circle, derivative, zeros or *roots,* and so on. With the topic in mind, use the questions below to help identify and create 3-D Viewer activities.

- *Algebraic*—What symbolism, notation, equations, and so on are important for your topic?
- *Graphic*—What graph or diagram conveys the topic's essence and makes it more visually concrete?
- *Numeric*—What data would display important topic patterns?

2. Select a dimension order for the 3-D Viewer perspectives. The strategy's full title, 3-D Viewer: Algebraic, Graphic, Numeric, clearly suggests the strategy's essential elements; however, the title intends no implication of a "proper" sequencing of the algebraic, graphic, and numeric elements. That is to say, for a given topic, there is no inherent reason that the algebraic viewpoint should be used first. Using 3-D Viewer requires using all three viewpoints, in any order, and then asking students to look at all three together to describe what each contributes to their understanding of the mathematics concept.

3. Create discussion questions to help students reflect on what each of the perspectives helps them see and understand about the topic. For example, "Which of the 3-D perspectives was most helpful to understanding the concept? Why?" or, "Explain what the graphic and numeric viewpoints *added* to your understanding of the topic that the algebraic does not."

4. Decide whether students will answer the questions individually or as members of small groups.

5. Plan time for whole-class discussion to share collectively the various insights into the mathematics concept.

Once students understand what each of the 3-D perspectives involves, you can have them generate their own algebraic, graphic, and numeric approaches to mathematics. One way to do this is to strategically direct students to employ a particular 3-D perspective. For example:

- "You have found an algebraic solution to that quadratic equation; now, verify your solution graphically (or numerically)."
- "In the function's graph, the line and circle appear to be tangent. Algebraically, prove that they are, or are not, tangent."
- "In your data table, the two ordered pairs (3, 2.1) and (4, −1.5) suggest the existence of a 'zero' between 3 and 4. Graph your data and estimate the value of the zero."

Another option is to provide a problem and allow students to generate their own 3-D solutions. For example:

- "Create your own example of a vertical line. Show algebraically, numerically, and graphically why your example is a vertical line."
- "Given that *y* varies inversely as *x*, and *y* equals 3 when *x* equals 2, use each of the 3-D Viewer perspectives to describe this function and its behaviors between 1 and 5."

If 3-D perspectives are new to your students, you'll need to model the different ways to represent mathematical concepts. For example, you can define the word *function* and add depth and dimension to the definition by showing how to represent a function:

- *Algebraically,* with a function rule mapping each x-value to a single y-value.
- *Graphically,* demonstrating how a graph of a function must pass the *vertical line test.*
- *Numerically,* using paired data to show that two ordered pairs can have the same y-value but not the same x-value.

Variations and Extensions

Using Technology

Technology is an obvious way to enhance and extend 3-D Viewer and, more generally, to build students' representational fluency. Teachers will find an abundance of technology tools that support visualization and that facilitate the representation and dynamic interactivity of the algebraic, graphic, and numeric. Likely, some useful technology tools that support 3-D Viewer are already in use in classrooms or are just a few clicks away on the Internet. Consider using the following resources:

- Textbook resources (e.g., publisher software, Web-based graphing ancillaries)
- Computer software (e.g., ZGrapher at www.brothersoft.com, graphing calculator at www.nucalc.com)
- Projection panels and SmartBoards
- Web-based graphing tools
- Graphing calculators

Modeling and Experimentation

Strategy Overview

In its purest sense, mathematics is highly abstract. For example, which of the following is the number 64, *(80 – 16)*, *LXIV*, *4³*, *128/2*, or *64*?

None of these is the number 64. These are all symbols that represent the number 64. Numbers in mathematics are only ideas; they cannot in and of themselves take on tangible or visible form. Now, which of the following is a line?

None of the figures shown is a line. What most people commonly call lines are only representations of a mathematical idea. In fact, in geometry, the term *line* is undefined. The points that form a line are infinitesimally small and have no size or shape. Therefore, true points and lines can never be seen.

Fortunately, in the real world, numbers can be represented or modeled by symbols or groups of objects, and lines can be represented symbolically and modeled by pictures drawn with a straight edge and a pencil. If we did not have our natural human ability to represent or model abstractions like numbers and lines, the process of learning and understanding mathematics would be extremely difficult. Math models help students to move past the simple notion that the study of mathematics is nothing more than facts and faith; models allow students to see, touch, experience, and manipulate math directly, so they can master its elements and appreciate its power. That's why the Modeling and Experimentation strategy puts such a high premium on translating and representing mathematical ideas using simple but well-selected models.

How to Use the Strategy & The Strategy in Action

There are many different ways to model mathematics. In this section, we describe five separate Modeling and Experimentation lessons. Each lesson includes a purpose, the materials needed, and step-by-step instructions for implementation. Each lesson is also tied to one of the five NCTM content standards. Here are the five lessons:

1. Basketball and Integers (Numbers and Operations standard)

2. Questions, Siblings, and Functions (Algebra standard)

3. Flags, Circles, and Rotations (Geometry standard)

4. Nets, 3-D Figures, and Surface Area (Measurement standard)

5. Probability and Dice (Data Analysis and Probability standard)

Understanding Integers (Numbers and Operations)

Activity: Basketball and Integers

Purpose: Students often struggle with integers, applying the wrong rules (or the right rules at the wrong time). The purpose of the Basketball and Integers activity is to use two basketball teams, competing against each other, as a model for combining integers. Once students experience the model and understand the connection to integers, the rules associated with integers will make sense and be much easier to remember and apply.

Materials: Two-sided counters (transparent and regular)

How to Implement the Model

1. Ask students if they've ever played basketball (or another sport) when one team had more players than the other. Invite them to share their stories.

2. Turn the overhead projector on, and place five red counters and two yellow counters on the glass.

3. Tell students that you are modeling a situation with two teams, one with red jerseys and the other yellow. Tell them that you are the referee getting ready to toss a jump ball. Ask them what they think a player from the yellow team would say. (Expected answer: Hey, this is not fair, the red team has more players than we do!)

4. Ask the students, between the two teams, which one has the advantage and by how many players? (Expected answer: The red team, by three players.)

5. Repeat for four yellow and two red, three red and two yellow, and five yellow and one red.

6. Place four red and four yellow on the glass, and ask which team has the advantage and by how many? Explain to students that in this case the answer will be *zero advantage* or simply *zero*.

7. Place four red on the glass, and then place two more red counters on the glass. Explain that four players showed up for the red team, then two more players for the red team came into the gym. No players for the yellow team came to play. Ask the students, "In this case, which teach has the advantage and by how many?" (Expected answer: The red team has the advantage by six.)

8. Next, tell students that you will provide team and player information in a different way. R4 and Y2 will represent four players for the red team and two players for the yellow team. Again, ask students which team has the advantage and by how many? Repeat this format for Y6 R5, Y1 R5, R4 Y4, R3 Y1, Y4 Y3, and R4 R2.

9. Next, tell students that you are going to change the names of the teams from yellow and red to positive and negative. Provide problems like –5 +8, +4 –5, –3 –2, and –7 +4. To work through the problems, continue using the question, Which team has the advantage and by how many?

10. Consider extensions. For example, you might model numbers with two leading signs with a scenario like this:

> The negative basketball team had two players on the floor and the positive team had three. Two more players from the negative team walked onto the floor but decided to change jerseys and play for the other team. At this point, which team had the advantage and by how many players?

This situation models the problem: –2 +3 – –2 = –2 +3 +2 = +3.

Understanding Functions (Algebraic Reasoning)

Activity: Questions, Siblings, and Functions

Purpose: The concept of a function is often confusing for students. Since all students know what it means to have brothers and sisters, the concept of siblings makes a great model for explaining functions while actively involving students in determining the critical attributes of an important concept.

Materials: White board or chalk board and student volunteers

How to Implement the Model

1. Ask for five student volunteers. Write their first names in an oval. Let the students know that they are all members of the *domain.*

2. Write the question, What are the names of your siblings? at the top center of the board. Draw a second oval to the right of the first. Tell students that this is where their answers will be written. Their answers to the question will be called the *range* (see Figure 3.7).

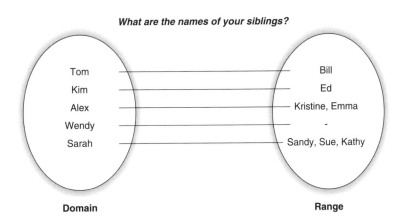

FIGURE 3.7 Not a Function

3. Tell the students that we are testing the question *What are the names of your siblings?* and determining if it represents a function or not. It all depends on the domain elements and their answers to the question.

4. Instruct students to take a look at the domain element *Tom* and note that he had one and only one answer, *Bill,* to the question. So far, the question qualifies as a function. *Kim* also answered the question with one and only one answer, *Ed.* This also satisfies the notion of function.

5. Next, check *Alex,* who had two answers to the question, What are the names of your siblings? Having more than one range answer is a violation of function; therefore, our question applied to our domain is *not* a function. Domain element *Sarah* also had more than one answer, which disqualifies the notion of function. Finally, domain element *Wendy* did not have any siblings and did not have an answer to the question, What are the names of your siblings? This also violates the notion of function.

The next step is to show how a closely related but different question produces a different result.

6. Use the same five student volunteers. Again, they will be members of the *domain.*

7. Change the question and write, How many siblings do you have? at the top center of the board. Again, a second oval to the right of the first will be used for the range, the answers to the question. This time, a survey of the members of the domain results in the answers *1, 1, 2, 0,* and *3* (see Figure 3.8). Note that this question, applied to the domain, resulted in one and only one answer for each domain element. Now we have a question that represents a function!

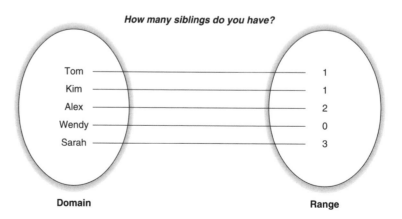

FIGURE 3.8 A Function!

8. At this point, it is important to connect functions in mathematics with the Questions, Siblings, and Functions Model. To make the connection, introduce the equation $f(x) = 2x + 1$. Tell students that this equation represents a question that can be asked of any domain number on the x-axis. What is the question? (The question represented by $f(x) = 2x + 1$ is *What is one more than twice your value?*)

9. Select five distinct, arbitrary number x values to form a domain. This is similar to selecting five students from class. Choose domain values {0, 1, 2, 5, and 10}.

10. Now ask the question, What is one more than twice your value? for each of the domain elements. The corresponding answers are {1, 3, 5, 11, and 21}. Since there's one and only one answer associated with each domain element, the equation $f(x) = 2x + 1$ does represent a function. Model a few more examples before asking students to try their hand at generating their own.

Understanding Rotations (Geometry and Spatial Sense)

Activity: Flags, Circles, and Rotations (Three Models)

Purpose: Transformations in geometry include translations, reflections, dilations, and rotations. For any point P(x,y), the supporting mathematics for translations, reflections, and dilations is simple algebra.

- To translate the point P(x,y) h units horizontally and v units vertically, simply plot the point P′$(x + h, y + v)$.
- To reflect the point P(x,y) across the x-axis, simply plot P′$(x,-y)$. To reflect P(x,y) across the y-axis, simply plot P′$(-x,y)$.
- To dilate the point P(x,y) by scale factor k, simply plot P′(kx, ky).

Visually, these transformations are relatively easy for students to see and understand. Rotations, on the other hand, require trigonometry and can be more difficult for students to grasp.

- To rotate the point P(x,y) θ degrees around the origin, plot P′$(x \cos \theta - y \sin \theta, y \cos \theta + x \sin \theta)$.

The three Modeling and Experimentation activities described below will help students to understand rotations of figures in the plane. Each shows a different way to model this concept.

Materials for Model 1:

- Graphing grid on white paper with x- and y-axes, four quadrants, and origin
- Straightened paper clip, one-inch flag cut from color paper, and transparent tape

- Two meter sticks, a paper flag, and masking tape
- A large protractor made for demonstrations at the white board or chalkboard

How to Implement Model 1

The rotation of an object in a plane always follows the path of a circle. To illustrate this to students, cut a flag from a sheet of construction paper, and tape it to the end of a meter stick. Using a second meter stick, form an angle by holding the ends of both sticks in one hand. Add a board protractor into the mix, and hold the pivot end of the meter sticks and the center point of the protractor together. Keep one meter stick horizontal and open the second stick clockwise, keeping the right ends together. Students will be able to see how the flag rotates in the plane around the origin as it rides the upper ray of the angle that is being opened according to the scale of the protractor. If the top meter stick closes in a counter-clockwise direction, the attached flag follows the path of a negative rotation around the operator's right hand (see Figure 3.9).

Students can model and experiment using a graphing grid on paper and a small cutout flag taped to a straightened paper clip. The end of the paper clip that does not contain the flag can rest at the origin. A small student-held protractor can be laid on the paper, and students can rotate their own flag varying degrees around the origin.

Materials for Model 2:

- Graphing grid on white paper with flag ABCDE drawn
- For each of the points A, B, C, D, and E, a circle drawn that has center (0,0) and contains the point
- A transparent overlay (transparency) with flag ABCDE drawn in the same position that it is drawn on the white paper
- A plastic-end bulletin board tack

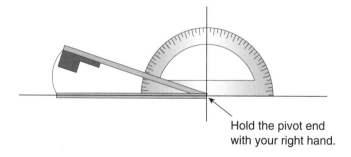

Hold the pivot end with your right hand.

FIGURE 3.9 Diagram of Meter-Stick Model

How to Implement Model 2

1. Issue each student a graphing grid with flag, and circles drawn. Issue each student a transparency with a congruent flag drawn.

2. Instruct students to overlay the transparency onto the white paper, so the two flags are superimposed identically.

3. Ask students to stick the tack through the transparency and into the origin of the graph on the white paper. A small piece of cardboard placed behind the origin behind the white paper will make this easy for students to do.

4. Invite students to experiment and rotate the transparency various multiples of 45 degrees. The blue guide lines and *x*- and *y*-axes divide the plane into 45-degree increments. As a vertex of the flag follows the path of a circle from one guide line to the next, the flag rotates 45 degrees (see Figure 3.10).

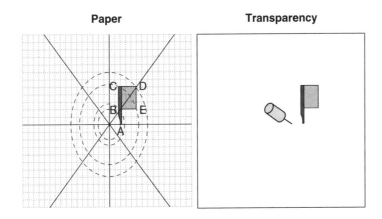

FIGURE 3.10   Diagram for Flag ABCDE Model

Materials for Model 3:

- Dimension 2000's Transformation Creation Software
- A picture, chosen by a student that includes rotations in its design; the picture can represent a real object or an artistic design

How to Implement Model 3

Transformation Creation (Thomas & Roe, 2009) is an executable program written in Java for both PC and Mac computers. It is marketed for schools and can be purchased from Dimension 2000 for standalone computers or as a site license. The program is designed to allow students to select various geometric shapes and functions, and apply translations, rotations, reflections, and dilations to them with the selection of appropriate buttons and the input of math data.

Through the use of color and shading tools, students can create a variety of pictures, simulations, and artistic designs. Figure 3.11 was created with repeated rotations of one function's graph in the Transformation Creation program.

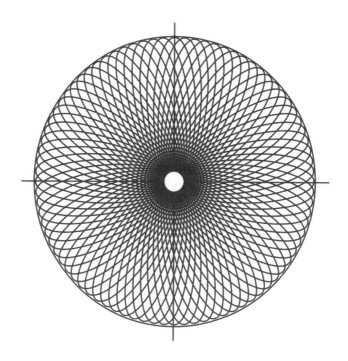

FIGURE 3.11   Image From Transformation Creation

Understanding Surface Area (Measurement)

Activity: Nets, 3-D Figures, and Surface Area

Purpose: The formulas for surface area of a rectangular prism and a cylinder are S.A. $_{\text{Rec Prism}}$ = $2\ell w + 2wh + 2\ell h$ and S.A. $_{\text{Cylinder}}$ = $2\,r^2 + 2\,rh$, respectively. Both of these formulas are lengthy and can be difficult for students to remember. The Nets, 3-D Figures, and Surface Area model challenges students to construct rectangular prisms and cylinders from scratch. This will help students to discover the breakdown and component parts of the three-dimensional figures and to learn how the areas of the parts relate to the surface area formulas of each whole figure. As a result of this activity, students will use their understanding of nets, three-dimensional figures, and surface area to actively construct the surface area formulas instead of simply memorizing them.

Materials: Cardstock, inch/centimeter ruler, scissors, tape, and instructions and specifications for constructing a rectangular prism and a cylinder

How to Implement the Model

1. Provide students with examples of rectangular prisms and cylinders, such as a cereal box and a cylindrical carton of salt.

2. Show students how a cereal box and salt carton can be cut and opened into flat pieces of cardboard that contain six rectangles, and one rectangle and two circles, respectively.

3. Provide students with cardstock, ruler, scissors, and tape, so they can create their three-dimensional models.

4. Draw a rectangular solid on the chalkboard or whiteboard.

5. Ask, "What would the drawing look like if the front face was opened and dropped down?" Draw and repeat for the other faces.

6. On the chalkboard or whiteboard, draw a net with measurements for a rectangular solid.

7. Have students use rulers and pencils to draw the net on cardstock. Ask that they label the measures of the lengths and widths of all six rectangles. Have them find the area of each rectangle and write the area measure in the center of each rectangle and circle the area measure.

8. Have students cut the net from the cardstock and fold along the edges to make the rectangular solid. Students can use scotch tape to connect the faces.

9. Ask students to total the areas of the component parts to derive the area of the three-dimensional figure.

10. Invite students to make connections between the construction activity and the formula for surface area of a rectangular prism.

11. Repeat the steps for creating and finding the surface area of a cylinder.

Note: You may also decide to display nets for three-dimensional figures using an overhead projector and have students draw their own nets using blank graph paper.

Nets for a rectangular solid and cylinder look like Figures 3.12 and 3.13 (p. 108).

Understanding Probability (Data Analysis and Probability)

Activity: Probability and Dice

Purpose: In the real world, games of chance are rarely fair, and without an understanding of the laws of probability and how the odds of winning can work for or against a player, students can be vulnerable. In this activity, students will work with a partner and play a game using dice. Students

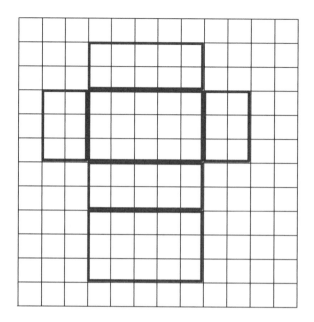

FIGURE 3.12 Net for Rectangular Solid

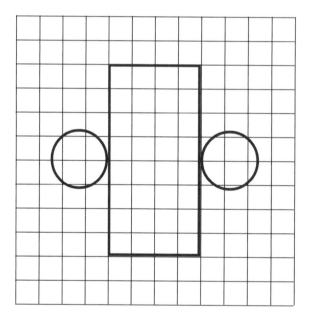

FIGURE 3.13 Net for Cylinder

will experience the consequences when the odds of winning favor only one of the two players. After playing the game, students will use the laws of probability to analyze the fairness of the game.

Materials: Each pair of students will need one pair of dice, paper, and pencils

How to Implement the Model

1. Pair your students and provide each pair of students with a pair of dice.

2. Designate students as Players A and B. Assign to Player A the word *odd*, and assign the word *even* to Player B.

3. Player A will start the game by rolling the dice. If the product of the two numbers rolled is an odd number, Player A receives 1 point. If the product is even, Player B earns 1 point. Player A cannot earn a point when the product is even, and Player B cannot earn a point when the product is odd.

4. After Player A rolls the dice and the point is assigned, Player B will roll the dice and a point will be assigned according to the odd-and-even rule. Students will take turns rolling the dice until one player reaches twenty points, at which time, the game is over. The player with the most points wins.

5. Let students play the game two or three times. Afterwards, ask how many A Players won. Ask how many B Players won. Students will learn that B Players won almost all the time.

6. Ask students to investigate why Player B had a greater chance of winning.

7. Work with students to create a table of possible paired outcomes. Use the paired outcomes and the laws of probability to show why it is always more likely that Player B will win this game.

The table shows a total of 36 possible products (Figure 3.14 on page 110). However, when one die is even, all six products are even. When one die is odd, three products are even and three products are odd. Thus, 27 out of 36 products in the sample space are even. Player B has a great advantage over Player A.

8. Challenge students to design a set of game rules that would put Player A at an even greater disadvantage as well as a set of game rules that would be fair for both players.

Why the Strategy Works

As with 3-D Viewer, Modeling and Experimentation is a strategy that builds students' representational fluency. What gives Modeling and Experimentation its special power is its ability to concretize the highly abstract concepts that make up much of the secondary mathematics curriculum. If difficult and abstract concepts are conveyed to students only through lectures, equations, formulas printed in textbooks, and black-and-white worksheets, then we can be certain that many students

Second Die / First Die	1	2	3	4	5	6
1	1	2	3	4	5	6
2	2	4	6	8	10	12
3	3	6	9	12	15	18
4	4	8	12	16	20	24
5	5	10	15	20	25	30
6	6	12	18	24	30	36

FIGURE 3.14   Products in the Paired Learner Dice Game

in our classrooms are not getting a firm grip on the mathematics they're learning. Modeling and Experimentation helps teachers cut through the abstraction associated with secondary mathematics through

- Real-world models that demonstrate mathematical ideas and concepts (as in the Basketball and Integers lesson);
- Interesting experiments that reveal mathematical patterns and concepts (as in the Probability and Dice lesson); and
- Hands-on activities that allow students to touch, manipulate, and create mathematical representations (as in the Nets, 3-D Figures, and Surface Area lessons).

Planning Considerations

1. As with any mathematics lesson, think about the fundamental understandings you want your students to acquire. Common examples are listed below.

- The properties of numbers, why they are needed, and what they mean.

- Fractions, the relationship between numerators and denominators, and operations between fractions.
- Integers and the rules for adding, subtracting, multiplying and dividing.
- Area formulas of plane figures and their subsequent role in surface area of three-dimensional figures.
- Properties of equality and their powerful role in solving equations.

2. Select a mathematical model, experiment, and/or hands-on experience that will clearly demonstrate the math concepts, math relationships, and outcomes you want your students to learn and understand. When developing a model to represent a math concept, take time to consider the degree of compatibility between the model and the mathematics. The notion of red and yellow basketball teams and advantages in terms of numbers of players has a high degree of compatibility with combining integers. On the other hand, that same model would not have a high degree of compatibility with fractions and mixed numbers, since teams don't consist of half a player, two thirds of a player, etc.

3. Determine the collaboration model that will work best for this activity. Will students need to work in pairs, groups of three or four, or individually?

4. Identify and collect the materials your students will need for the modeling and experimentation activity. Determine how and when the materials will be distributed to students and how they will be collected at the end of the activity.

5. Be prepared to demonstrate those parts of the activity that students may need help with. Do your students know how to use the math tools needed for this activity? It is usually best to wait until the demonstration is completed and questions have been answered before distributing materials to students.

6. Make plans to connect the math learned in the hands-on activity with the abstract representation of math students will see in textbooks and on high-stakes tests. For example, as students answer questions about the red team and yellow team in the Basketball and Integers model, they should also be asked to simplify problems like $-7 + 5$, so they are sure to connect the idea *Which team has more, and by how many?* with the concept of combining integers. Connections should occur during the modeling and hands-on activity, not only afterwards.

7. Determine if a visual organizer or written instructions will need to be created to help students succeed in the activity.

8. Determine how you will assess the success of the Modeling and Experimentation activity. Will students be asked to write or talk about

their new understandings? Will they need to demonstrate their understanding on a quiz, test, or project?

9. Because learning takes time, be prepared and willing to *pull the model out of the closet* as needed. Even though students may connect the model to the math on the day of the activity, several days later they may forget the connection.

Variations and Extensions

An important variation is student-created modeling in which you challenge students to develop and demonstrate models to represent mathematical concepts. Note that student-created models reverse the thinking process. Instead of learning abstract ideas via models, students are charged with taking abstract ideas they've already learned and coming up with concrete ways to represent those ideas.

Inductive Learning

Strategy Overview

Too often in mathematics classrooms, students learn—or, more accurately, memorize—vocabulary, formulas, properties, and algorithms all without a clear understanding of the big picture or conceptual categories into which these mathematical elements fit. Without this all-important big picture, mathematics can seem to students a hodgepodge of unrelated facts with no conceptual "glue" to bind together what they are learning. Instead, each topic becomes just another set of disjointed *math stuff* to memorize rather than an expansion of knowledge or a new layer of understanding added to a what's been previously learned.

The Inductive Learning strategy helps students to develop a broad conceptual understanding of mathematical topics while they develop critical-thinking skills. The model for the strategy comes from the influential work of Hilda Taba (1971), who discovered that student abilities to see big ideas and make generalizations could be greatly improved through a three-part inductive process in which students:

1. *Examine a set of data.* For example, students might be provided with a randomly organized collection of two-dimensional figures: square, hexagon, scalene triangle, and so on.

2. *Organize the terms into meaningful groups, and give each group a descriptive label.* For example, students might create a group called four-sided shapes and include square, rectangle, rhombus, trapezoid, and kite.

3. *Make predictions about the topic, which they monitor and revise as they acquire new information.* For example, students might make these predictions about the upcoming unit:
   - We will review how to find area and perimeter.
   - We will learn about the differences between the different types of triangles.

How to Use the Strategy

1. Present to students (or work with students to establish) the key vocabulary terms, mathematical expressions, or thinking words that demonstrate the key concepts. Try to mix the familiar with the unfamiliar.

2. Model the group-and-label process. Modeling is especially important for students who are new to the group-and-label process. Once a class has experienced the process a few times, modeling may not be necessary.

3. Divide students into small groups, and ask them to review the terms and then organize them into meaningful groups.

4. Instruct students to create a simple but descriptive label for each group that explains what the terms or expressions in the group have in common. Unless explicitly restricted, students may place words and terms in more than one group.

5. Ask students to use their groups to make two or three generalizations or predictions about the topic.

6. Ask students to collect information over the course of the lesson or unit that supports or refutes their generalizations and predictions.

7. Build in time for reflection, self-assessment, and practice, so students learn how to group and label on their own.

Note: Some mathematics teachers may be strongly inclined to "tell" their students what connections they might look for. The typical teacher concern is that students will not see the right things on their own and get it wrong. This tendency impedes student thinking. Students should be encouraged to search for and articulate connections without constraints! Students may not, indeed students need not, see the patterns the teacher sees—at least initially. Inductive Learning will help students develop the habit of looking for patterns without the ever-present mathematics notion of the "right answer." Once students have grouped and labeled according to their insights, group or class discussions of similarities and differences of groups will help students to test and revise their understanding. Then, as the lesson or unit progresses, students will continue to make revisions in light of new learning. Revising their groups and their generalizations in this way actively engages students in constructing meaning—an ideal state for in-depth learning.

The Strategy in Action

Inductive Learning lessons can be of three types: term based, expression based, and thinking based. Examples of all three types follow.

Term-Based Inductive Learning

This use of the strategy focuses on the critical terms in a unit of study.

Seventh-grade teacher Gina Nuernberger selects the important vocabulary words from her next unit on statistics. She knows that some words will be familiar to students and that others will be new to them.

arithmetic average	*bar graph*	*box-and-whisker plot*
cluster	*frequency table*	*tally*
graph	*interval*	*line graph*

line plot   *mean*   *median*

mode   *range*   *scale*

scatter plot   *stem-and-leaf plot*

Gina forms small teams of students and distributes to each team the set of vocabulary words (above) and a Group and Label organizer containing ovals for groups and rectangles for labels (Figure 3.15 below). Gina asks each team to study the set of words, use their glossaries to look up the meanings of new words, make a team decision about how to group words into the ovals of the organizer, and write a descriptive label in the rectangle immediately below each group. Gina also gives some additional guidelines for grouping the words:

- There must be at least three groups.
- Each group must contain at least three terms.
- Terms can be placed in more than one group.

Here's how one group organized the terms:

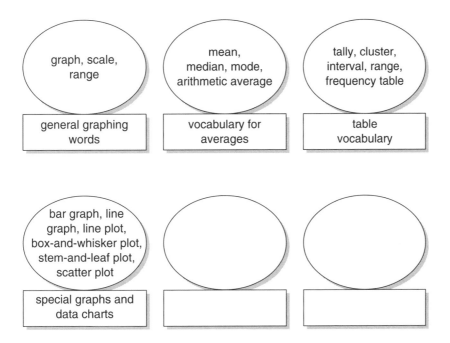

FIGURE 3.15 Student Team's Group and Label Organizer

Once the individual teams complete grouping and labeling, Gina invites each group to explain their classification system. Once all groups present and explain their groups and the thinking behind them, Gina leads a class discussion in which she helps students identify those terms that the class as a whole seems to understand well and those that gave them trouble. Before beginning the unit, Gina asks students to make some predictions about how graphing and statistics might be related. Students come up with several ideas:

- Graphing is how you show statistical information.
- Graphing makes it easier to understand statistics.
- Statisticians use a variety of graphing tools.
- Different kinds of graphs are good for different kinds of statistical information.

Gina asks students to write three predictions down the middle column of a Support and Refute organizer that looks like Figure 3.16.

As the unit progresses, Gina asks students to revisit their organizers and record any new information they've learned that either supports or refutes their predictions.

Support	Prediction	Refute
	Graphing is how you show statistical information.	
	Statisticians use many graphing tools.	
	Different kinds of graphs are good for different kinds of statistical information.	

FIGURE 3.16 Support and Refute Organizer for Graphing

Expression-Based Inductive Learning

This use of the strategy asks students to examine, group, and label actual mathematical expressions or geometric shapes that demonstrate key ideas.

Dan Bloch's algebra students have been learning to use the various equation properties of equality. Before his students sharpen their equation-solving skills, Dan wants his students to be able to discriminate among the various equation types, so he assembles a collection of 21 equations, almost all of which involve decimals.

Students pair up to look over the equations and group them into at least four sets based on three criteria:

1. Each equation must be placed in one and only one group.

2. Each group must have at least three equations.

3. You must be able to explain in one sentence the reason for your grouping.

A sample student grouping appears in Figure 3.17.

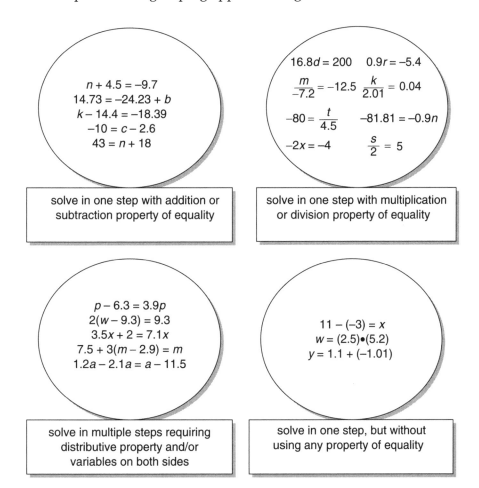

FIGURE 3.17 Sample Grouping and Labeling of Equations

Afterwards, Dan leads a class discussion in which he and his students develop some generalizations:

- While an endless number of equations can be created, just four operations—addition, subtraction, multiplication, and division—are used to combined terms and simplify.
- Variables can be on either or both sides of an equation.
- Keeping the order of operations in mind is useful in classifying equations.
- The more complicated equation is one that involves a quantity. The distributive property is likely to be useful in such cases.

Once students see clearly the importance of the four basic operations and that a few rules and properties are central to solving equations, Dan moves forward with the unit. Over the course of the unit, as students encounter increasingly complex equations, Dan invites students to reflect on their observations to see if they can add anything new or make any revisions to their thinking.

Thinking-Based Inductive Learning

This use of the strategy assembles "thinking words," or words related to the thinking processes, that students will use in a unit, or as in the lesson below, over the course of an entire unit.

During the first week of pre-algebra, Ariana Radford presents a list of 36 "problem-solving" words to her students, words like *divide, least, equal, multiple, solve, product, difference,* and so on.

Ariana wants her students to see that mathematical problem solving is really made up of only a few related thinking processes. So, she begins by having students examine the words, review new words, start to put words together, and create descriptive headings for each group. Figure 3.18 shows an example.

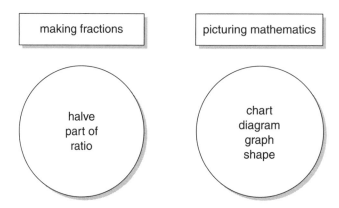

FIGURE 3.18 Initial Headings and Groups

After students have formed their groups, Ariana works with them to develop a few generalizations about thinking algebraically. Generalizations range from the general to the specific:

- *General:* Algebra requires figuring out what kind of thinking you need to use before you solve a problem.
- *Specific:* In algebra, you can represent math ideas with visual or picture formats like graphs and charts.

Over the course of the year, as students' exposure to new kinds of problems increases, Ariana and the students revise their generalizations and expand their groups by adding words to old groups and creating new groups to accommodate new understanding.

Why the Strategy Works

Induction, or moving from the specific to the general, is a natural thinking process. When confronted with multiple pieces of specific information, the human brain is designed to look for something that connects them, a thread of meaning, a big idea or generalization. For example, have you ever played the game "Which one doesn't belong?" Let's try a game right now. Below are six common household items (Figure 3.19). Which one doesn't belong?

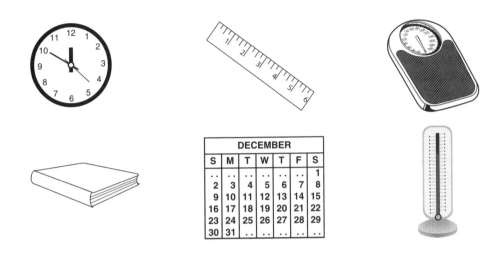

FIGURE 3.19 Common Household Items

The great majority of people will identify the book as the misfit because their brains figure out in pretty short order that a clock, a ruler, a bathroom scale, a calendar, and a thermometer all have measurement in common.

Let's try another one. Here are five office supplies (Figure 3.20). Which one doesn't belong and why?

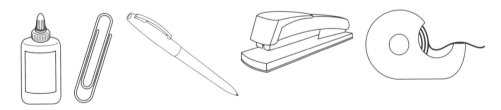

FIGURE 3.20 Common Office Supplies

Now, let's really put your brain's power to think inductively to the test. From the same five office supplies above, identify a different item that you could remove based on a different way of thinking about what all the items have in common.

Here are some different ideas that others have come up with:

- Remove the pen because all the others hold things together.

- Remove the paperclip because all the others run out or need to be refilled.
- Remove the glue because all the others contain metal or have sharp points.

So, what happens when we put this human drive for making meaning through induction to work in the classroom? That's what Hilda Taba (1971) set out to discover. She found that asking students to examine terms or data, group and label the terms, and use their groups to form hypotheses, predictions, or generalizations led to

- Increased responsibility for learning among students;
- Improved analytical and interpretive skills; and
- Yielded deeper insights into how the big ideas and details, which make up lessons and units, fit together.

Recently, the research community has caught up with Taba and her inductive teaching model. The two core thinking processes that drive Inductive Learning are classification, or grouping information according to common attributes, and generating and testing hypotheses, which students engage in when they make their predictions and modify them as they acquire new information. Both of these thinking processes have been identified as two of the surest ways to raise student achievement levels (Marzano, 2007; Marzano, Pickering, Pollock, 2001).

Planning Considerations

Use the following steps to plan a successful Inductive Learning lesson:

1. Identify a mathematical topic and the key concepts that will be encountered in the lesson or unit. There's a saying we use for people who miss the big picture and instead get lost in the details. We say that person "can't see the forest for the trees." Inductive Learning will not only help students take a broad view that helps reveal the forest but it also increases their ability to see the relationships between one tree and the others. Because of its focus on the structure of content, Inductive Learning is ideal for introducing a new unit, classifying vocabulary words, or for reviewing (by reinforcing an organizing structure that supports retention). Your first task is to identify those important key concepts that you expect students to discover.

2. Select 15 to 30 topic-related or concept-related elements that need to be understood as part of deep understanding. Such mathematics elements can be terms, expressions, properties, procedures, graphs, and so on. For example, to introduce a unit on polygons, Kelly Krause provided her students with a vocabulary list filled with both familiar and unfamiliar terms: *angle, circle, decagon, diagonal, dodecagon, heptagon, hexagon, hypotenuse, line, octagon, parallelogram, pentagon, point, quadrilateral, rectangle, right triangle, segment, side,* and *triangle.*

Another teacher who used Inductive Learning to help students review the concepts *factors, multiples, greatest common factor* and *least common multiple* chose the following expressions (see Figure 3.21). (For the actual lesson, the expressions were randomized, of course!)

Factors	**Multiples**
For 36 _____ is/are {1, 2, 3, 4, 6, 9, 12, 18, 36}	For 9 _____ is/are {9, 18, 27, ...}
For 9 _____ is/are {1, 3, 9}	For 15 _____ is/are {15, 30, 45, ...}
For 100 _____ is/are {1, 2, 3, 4, 5, 10, 20, 25, 50, 100}	For 12 _____ is/are {12, 24, 36, ...}
For 60 _____ is/are {1, 2, 3, 4, 5, 6, 10, 12, 15, 20, 30, 60}	For 7 _____ is/are {7, 14, 21, ...}
For 2 _____ is/are {1, 2}	For 10 _____ is/are {10, 20, 30, ...}
For 7 _____ is/are {1, 7}	For 5 _____ is/are {5, 10, 15, ...}
For 13 _____ is/are {1, 13}	
Greatest Common Factor	**Least Common Multiple**
For 2 and 6 _____ is/are 2	For 2 and 8 _____ is/are 8
For 3 and 4 _____ is/are 1	For 4 and 6 _____ is/are 12
For 15 and 20 _____ is/are 5	For 2 and 5 _____ is/are 10
For 6 and 15 _____ is/are 3	For 4 and 5 _____ is/are 20
For 2 and 6 _____ is/are 2	For 2 and 6 _____ is/are 6
For 6 and 8 _____ is/are 2	For 6 and 15 _____ is/are 30
For 6 and 5 _____ is/are 1	For 6 and 8 _____ is/are 24
For 6 and 9 _____ is/are 3	For 6 and 9 _____ is/are 18
For 4 and 12 _____ is/are 4	
For 8 and 12 _____ is/are 4	

FIGURE 3.21　Groups of Mathematical Statements

Keep in mind a few guidelines for building lists of concept elements:

- Individual elements must be specific, not vague or general.
- Since elements will be grouped, lists should contain three or more elements related to a given concept.
- If an Inductive Learning lesson is used to introduce a unit, it is very important to include a majority of familiar terms so that students can confidently form at least some logical groups. This will set the stage for connecting the unknown to the known.

3. Design or adapt an appropriate grouping and labeling organizer, or empower students to create one of their own. Organizers provide visual support as students arrange and keep track of related information. A Group and Label organizer can be a very simple arrangement of circles or ovals for groups and narrow rectangles for labels.

4. Determine whether the activity will be completed by each individual student, by groups of students, or both at different points of the activity. Student thinking, small group collaboration, and whole-class discussion all take time and should not be rushed. For example, when Kelly Krause uses Inductive Learning for an end-of-unit review, she frequently requires each student to group and label on his or her own. Kelly then pairs students and asks them to exchange their individual organizational thoughts and develop a shared graphic representation.

5. Prepare a set of questions that will provoke deep thinking. Forming groups according to their own perception may be a new idea to many students, so they will probably need both encouragement and support. Teacher modeling will be important, but beyond that, teachers should prepare questions that will encourage students to explore connections and make associations that might be missed initially. Questions that compel students to think more deeply about their groups sound like this:

- What other elements might fit that group?
- Another student formed a group of these four terms: ___, ___, ___, ___. What connection do you think that student was thinking about?
- If I used the label ___, what terms would fit in the group?
- If you remove ___ from your group, what change would you make in your label?
- Did you consider grouping these items based upon their algebraic, geometric, or numerical similarities?

6. Develop a synthesis task. How will students apply what they have learned? All Inductive Learning activities lend themselves to synthesis opportunities. Here are a few ideas:

- Create a new organizer different from the one we used during the lesson that would dramatically emphasize the concepts you discovered.
- Draw three classroom chalkboards, one for each concept, that contain the mathematics needed to understand each concept.
- Write a one-paragraph summary of each concept you uncovered with your groups and labels.

4

Interpersonal Strategies

OVERVIEW

Interpersonal strategies help students *discuss* mathematical ideas, *collaborate* to solve problems, and *explore the human connections* to mathematical content.

Interpersonal math students . . .

- *Want to* learn math through dialogue, collaboration, and cooperative learning.
- *Like math problems that* focus on real-world applications and on how mathematics helps people.
- *Approach problem solving* as an open discussion among a community of problem solvers.
- *Experience difficulty when* instruction focuses on independent seatwork or when what they are learning seems to lack real-world application.
- *Want a math teacher who* pays attention to their successes and struggles in mathematics.

The four Interpersonal strategies in this chapter can help you meet these NCTM Process Standards.

Strategy	NCTM Process Standards*				
	Problem Solving	Reasoning and Proof	Communication	Connections	Representation
Reciprocal Learning [p. 125] Students work together in pairs on parallel tasks; each student works as a player/doer who completes the activity and as a coach/guide who provides clues, encouragement, and feedback to ensure a successful outcome.			✓	✓	
Collaborative Summarizing [p. 136] Students work together to discuss and negotiate a list of the most important ideas they've identified from the content, so they can collaboratively construct a powerful summary.	✓		✓	✓	✓
Game Competition [p. 141] Students practice key skills, review essential concepts, and improve their understanding of the content by competing with and against other students in a variety of game formats.			✓	✓	✓
Paired Learner & Cooperative Learning [p. 150] Students work together in pairs (or in groups of three or four) to complete an activity as they support each other's learning.		✓	✓	✓	

FIGURE 4.0 Correlation of Interpersonal Strategies to NCTM Process Standards

*For more information on the National Council of Teachers of Mathematics (NCTM) Process Standards, please consult their *Principles and Standards for School Mathematics* (2000), or visit their website at www.nctm.org.

Reciprocal Learning

Strategy Overview

In the world of sports, players and participants depend on their coaches to observe their performance, make suggestions for improvement, and increase their motivation. Players learn to count on their coach to provide discipline, support, and encouragement. The role of the coach is integral to the practice and training routines that help players master athletic skills. The power of the coach and player relationship is captured by the Reciprocal Learning strategy.

Reciprocal Learning can effectively double the power of student learning by requiring each member of a learning pair to play both roles in the player-coach relationship. As a *player*, the student completes a set of math activities or exercises provided by the teacher. In this role, the student should try to think out loud—to expose his or her internal thinking process to the coach while completing the exercises. As a *coach*, the student listens to the player, provides encouragement, feedback, praise, and helpful tips towards completing the exercises when the player gets stuck. The coach must not give the answers to the player. Instead, the coach should try to lead the player to the answers.

Central to the Reciprocal Learning strategy are specially designed worksheets that look like Figure 4.1. (Notice how the answers to Player A's questions are on Player B's sheet and vice versa. This is because, while Player A is answering the questions, Player B is coaching Player A to the correct answers.)

Player A's Sheet

Player A's Questions	Answers to Player B's Questions and Coaching Hints
1. State the *order of operations*. 2. In algebra, a placeholder is called a _____ . 3. What is an *algebraic expression*? 4. Define and give an example of the *commutative property* of addition and multiplication. 5. What property is being shown in the equation . . .	1. The *distributive property* ties multiplication and division together by allowing you to break apart factors into a sum. For example: $7(1 + 3) = 7 \bullet 1 + 7 \bullet 3$ 2. Terms with the same variables are called *like terms*. Example: $5x + 7x$ 3. $12y + 5$ is in simplest form because it has no like terms and no parentheses.

(Continued)

(Continued)

Player B's Sheet

Player B's Questions	Answers to Player A's Questions and Coaching Hints
1. What property ties multiplication and addition together? How?	1. Order of operations
	1. Do parentheses first.
2. When terms have the same variable, they are called _____. Give an example.	2. Do exponents next.
	3. Do multiplication and division from left to right.
3. Is the expression $12y + 5$ in simplest form? How do you know?	4. Do addition and subtraction from left to right. Remember: PEMDAS (Please Excuse My Dear Aunt Sally)
4. Define an equation. Give an example.	2. A placeholder is called a *variable* because the value can vary or change.
5. When an equation has a variable . . .	3. An algebraic expression is a combination of variables, numbers . . .

FIGURE 4.1 Reciprocal Learning Worksheets (Excerpted)

How to Use the Strategy

1. Using the blank Reciprocal Learning Worksheets that appear at the end of this strategy (Organizers D and E on pages 134 and 135), create a set of Reciprocal Learning Worksheets to distribute to each student pair.

2. Break students into pairs and explain the role of player and coach to students. It is always a good idea to model the behaviors of good players (e.g., thinking aloud, perseverance) and coaching (e.g., providing praise and encouragement, guiding the player without providing answers).

3. Instruct Player A to work through the exercises on his sheet while the coach uses the Coach's Hints on her sheet to help Player A to the answers.

4. Have students reverse roles: Player A becomes the coach, while the coach becomes Player B. Player B then works through the exercises on her sheet while Player A coaches her.

5. You may choose to include a cooperative challenge for students to solve together after they have both served as player and coach.

6. Over time, encourage students to use the peer-coaching structure of Reciprocal Learning as their own review and practice strategy.

The Strategy in Action

Neela Rezvani uses Reciprocal Learning regularly in her classroom for four reasons:

1. Reciprocal Learning helps her students practice and develop their mathematical skills.

2. It provides her with good, consistent formative-assessment information. By observing student pairs as they work, Neela gets a snapshot of students' learning—what skills they've mastered, what skills need development, and how their comprehension of key concepts is growing.

3. It helps students develop important social skills and habits: active listening, providing constructive feedback, trust, patience, and positive encouragement.

4. It sets the tone for Neela's classroom. By using Reciprocal Learning regularly, students come to understand that the classroom is a positive environment where all students help each other learn.

Today, Neela is using Reciprocal Learning to help her students review and practice what they have been learning recently: how to find the surface area of a rectangular solid.

After students break up into pairs, Neela distributes the Reciprocal Learning Worksheets (Figures 4.2 and 4.3) to each pair of students. For the players, Neela provides three basic problems in which all the values are provided, along with two simple word problems that require students to set up the problem. To increase her students' fluency with different units of measurement, Neela writes the problems so that they include a variety of units: centimeters, inches, and feet.

For the coaches, Neela provides more than just the answers. She also provides the formula, tips and hints, reminders ("use the vocabulary"), sample questions the coach can use to help expose the player's thinking process, and the steps in solving the five problems.

Finding the Surface Area of a Rectangular Solid

Player A's Problems	Coach's Notes for Player B

For each problem, *find the surface area of the rectangular figures* described below.
 	
1) $\ell = 10$ in, $w = 5$ in, and $h = 3$ in.
 	
2) $\ell = 30$ in, $w = 15$ in, and $h = 9$ in.
 	
3) $\ell = 8.5$ cm, $w = 2.0$ cm, and $h = 4.0$ cm.
 	
4) A shoebox has a width of 6 inches. The length of the shoebox is twice its width, and its height is two inches less than its width.
 	
5) A rectangular storage container has a square bottom that is one-half foot on a side. The container is four times taller than it is wide.
	Encourage your partner to
	
	• Sketch *and* label the solid.
	• Think out loud using questions like:
	  ○ How do you take half of something?
	  ○ Instead of writing ½ as a fraction, how else could you write it? As a decimal? Which do you like better?
	  ○ When you multiply three numbers together (step b in the solution), does the order of multiplication matter?
	  ○ When you add three numbers together (step c in the solution), does the order matter?
	• Use the vocabulary.
	• For each problem, write the general surface area formula: $SA = 2\ell w + 2hw + 2\ell h$
	• Carefully show in writing the substitution of variables' values into the SA formula *and* each step to the answer.
	• Include units with the numerical answer.
	
	Answers
	
	1) $SA = 2\ell w + 2hw + 2\ell h$
	  a. $SA = 2(12)(4) + 2(6)(4) + 2(12)(6)$
	  b. $SA = 96 + 48 + 144$
	  c. $SA = 288$ sq ft
	
	2) $SA = 2\ell w + 2hw + 2\ell h$
	  a. $SA = 2(6)(2) + 2(3)(2) + 2(6)(3)$
	  b. $SA = 24 + 12 + 36$
	  c. $SA = 72$ sq ft
	
	3) $SA = 2\ell w + 2hw + 2\ell h$
	  a. $SA = 2(4)(8) + 2(1.5)(8) + 2(4)(1.5)$
	  b. $SA = 64 + 24 + 12$
	  c. $SA = 100$ sq in.
	
	4) $SA = 2\ell w + 2hw + 2\ell h$
	  a. $SA = 2(30)(18) + 2(10)(18) + 2(30)(10)$
	  b. $SA = 1080 + 360 + 600$
	  c. $SA = 2040$ sq in.
	
	5) $SA = 2\ell w + 2hw + 2\ell h$
	  a. $SA = 2(8)(4) + 2(2)(4) + 2(8)(2)$
	  b. $SA = 64 + 16 + 32$
	  c. $SA = 112$ sq cm

FIGURE 4.2 Reciprocal Learning Worksheet for Player A

Finding the Surface Area of a Rectangular Solid

Player B's Problems	Coach's Notes for Player A

For each problem, *find the surface area of the rectangular solid* described below.
 	
1) $\ell = 12$ ft, $w = 4$ ft, and $h = 6$ ft
 	
2) $\ell = 6$ ft, $w = 2$ ft, and $h = 3$ ft
 	
3) $\ell = 4$ in., $w = 8$ in., and $h = 1.5$ in.
 	
4) A rectangular suitcase has a height of 10 inches. Its length is three times its height. Its depth is 8 inches more than the height.
 	
5) A tiny, dollhouse-sized brick is 8 centimeters long. The brick's width is half of its length, and its height is just a quarter of its length.
	Encourage your partner to
	
	• Sketch *and* label the solid.
	• Think out loud using questions like:
	  ○ How do you take half of something?
	  ○ Instead of writing ½ as a fraction, how else could you write it? As a decimal? Which do you like better?
	  ○ When you multiply three numbers together (step b in the solution), does the order of multiplication matter?
	  ○ When you add three numbers together (step c in the solution), does the order matter?
	• Use the vocabulary.
	• For each problem, write the general surface area formula: $SA = 2\ell w + 2hw + 2\ell h$
	• Carefully show in writing the substitution of variables' values into the SA formula *and* each step to the answer.
	• Include units with the numerical answer.
	
	Answers
	
	1) $SA = 2\ell w + 2hw + 2\ell h$
	  a. $SA = 2(10)(5) + 2(3)(5) + 2(10)(3)$
	  b. $SA = 100 + 30 + 60$
	  c. $SA = 190$ sq in.
	
	2) $SA = 2\ell w + 2hw + 2\ell h$
	  a. $SA = 2(30)(15) + 2(9)(15) + 2(30)(9)$
	  b. $SA = 900 + 270 + 540$
	  c. $SA = 1710$ sq in.
	
	3) $SA = 2\ell w + 2hw + 2\ell h$
	  a. $SA = 2(8.5)(2) + 2(4)(2) + 2(8.5)(4)$
	  b. $SA = 34 + 16 + 68$
	  c. $SA = 118$ sq cm
	
	4) $SA = 2\ell w + 2hw + 2\ell h$
	  a. $SA = 2(12)(6) + 2(4)(6) + 2(12)(4)$
	  b. $SA = 144 + 48 + 96$
	  c. $SA = 288$ sq in.
	
	5) $SA = 2\ell w + 2hw + 2\ell h$
	  a. $SA = 2(0.5)(0.5) + 2(0.5)(2) + 2(2)(0.5)$
	  Or
	  $SA = 2(\frac{1}{2})(\frac{1}{2}) + 2(\frac{1}{2})(2) + 2(2)(\frac{1}{2})$
	  b. $SA = 0.5 + 2 + 2$
	  c. $SA = 4.5$ sq ft

FIGURE 4.3 Reciprocal Learning Worksheet for Player B

As students work together, Neela moves around the room to observe and listen in on the partnerships. When players are struggling, Neela works with the coach, helping the coach to expose the player's thinking process and guide the player to the answers. Once all students have completed their problems, Neela presents pairs with a cooperative challenge, which they solve together:

> On Sheet A, one set of values for l, w, and h is twice the other. On sheet B, one set of values is three times the other. What happens to the total surface area when you double or triple the values of l, w, and h? Can you figure out how you can exactly double and exactly triple the total surface area?

To synthesize the lesson, Neela asks students to reflect on what they've learned *and* on their performance as both player and coach. She then leads a discussion in which students share ideas for how they can improve as players and as coaches for the next Reciprocal Learning lesson.

Why the Strategy Works

There is a large body of research highlighting the instructional benefits of student learning partnerships. Students who work in learning partnerships spend more time working on task, develop more positive attitudes towards learning, and make measurable academic gains (King-Sears & Bradley, 1995). What's more, the research of Fuchs, Fuchs, Mathes, and Simmons (1997) has shown that the increases in academic intensity associated with learning partnerships need not cut into instructional time.

What makes Reciprocal Learning such an effective way to design student-learning partnerships is the player-coach relationship that sits at its center. As players work through problems, they are reminded by their coach that mathematical problem solving is not a pencil-and-paper process; it is a thinking process that players must articulate. To serve as coaches, on the other hand, students must pay close attention to what the player is doing and thinking—and use positive coaching behaviors to help the player identify and correct errors. By playing both of these roles, students develop new perspectives on teaching and learning, while their mathematical skills are doubly reinforced.

Planning Considerations

To plan a quality Reciprocal Learning lesson you need to:

1. Determine the focus of the lesson. Reciprocal Learning is well suited to reviewing content and mastering skills and procedures. It works equally well whether you want students to review the key terms in a unit on measures of central tendency, practice finding mean, median, and mode—or both.

2. Design worksheets. For the Reciprocal Learning lesson, you'll need to design two worksheets: one for all Player As in the partnership and another for all Player Bs. Remember that each worksheet contains the player's problems and coaching material for when the player switches roles and becomes the other player's coach (see Figures 4.2 and 4.3 on pages 128–129 for models).

> Remember, coaches need more than just answers. They also need hints and tips that will help them guide the player to these answers. Provide the coach with necessary formulas, examples, memory refreshers, or any other information they can use to assist the player.
>
> You may also choose to include a cooperative challenge on the worksheets. Cooperative challenges provide a good way to keep partnerships that finish early actively engaged while other partnerships complete their work. Student pairs need only one cooperative challenge because they will work on it together once they have completed the player-coach portions of their worksheets. Here's a creative cooperative challenge designed by a teacher for a Reciprocal Learning lesson on mathematical properties:
>
> *Cooperative Challenge:* Pick the term from the worksheets that you believe is the most important. Develop a metaphor that compares this term to something else. Explain your metaphor.

3. Decide how you and students will manage the lesson. Below are some questions to consider.

- How will partnerships be assigned? Whatever method you choose, make sure that students change partners in successive lessons. This sends an important message—namely, that all students are expected to work together.
- How will you explain and model effective player and coach behaviors?
- How will the classroom be arranged? Partnerships work best when students sit side by side rather than head to head.

Variations and Extensions

Peer Problem Solving

Peer Problem Solving has proven highly successful in developing problem-solving skills (Whimbey & Lochhead, 1999). Peer Problem Solving applies the player-coach format of Reciprocal Learning to more involved, nonroutine problems. For example, Figure 4.4 shows the problems, answers, and coaching hints a teacher provided to student pairs for a Peer Problem Solving lesson.

Partner A's Problem

A farmer has some land that is to be divided equally among his four children into four parcels. His land is shown below. The parcels must be the same shape and size. Draw the four parcels on the figure below.

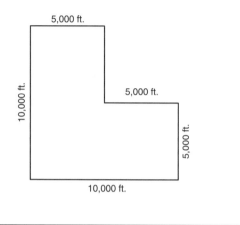

5,000 ft.

10,000 ft.

5,000 ft.

5,000 ft.

10,000 ft.

Partner B's Problem

You have eight balls, all of which look exactly the same. Seven of them weigh the same, but one is slightly lighter than the others. You have a scale to balance the balls. How can you find out which is the lighter ball in only two weighings?

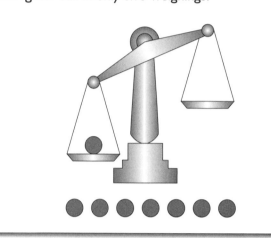

Hints and Answers to Partner A's Problem

Hints

A. Suggest that your partner consider dividing the property into three equal parts

B. Then, divide each of three parcels into four smaller parts.

C. Have your partner count the total number of smaller parts (there should be 12). Next, tell your partner to divide the 12 parts by 4 since there are 4 children.

D. Finally, have your partner arrange the little parts in such a way that all of the children receive a parcel of the same shape.

Hints and Answers to Partner B's Problem

Hints

1. Most people try to weigh all eight balls at once.

2. How can you figure out which is lightest if you only have three balls?

Answer

1. Weigh six balls (three on each side).

2. If they weigh the same, then the lighter ball must be one of the two balls not weighed. Weigh the remaining two balls to see which is lighter.

3. If the three balls from Step 1 are of different weights, weigh two of the three balls that were on the lighter side. If they weigh the same, the ball that is left is the lighter ball. If one weighs less, you have found the lighter ball.

FIGURE 4.4 Peer Problem Solving

Source: Silver, H. F., Strong, R. W., & Perini, M. J. (2007). *The Strategic Teacher: Selecting the Right Research-Based Strategy for Every Lesson.* (p. 171).

To facilitate the higher-order thinking that Peer Problem Solving requires, follow these six steps:

1. Ask all coaches to look over their player's problem and its solution.

2. Have all coaches meet together to form two coaches' groups. Encourage coaches to discuss the problem, follow the steps, and make sure they understand how to arrive at the solution.

3. Instruct coaches to generate any additional ideas or steps they think might be helpful to the player.

4. Form partnerships. One student becomes the problem solver, while the other serves as the coach.

5. Remind players to think out loud, and encourage coaches to listen carefully to the player's thinking and use the coaching tips and what they learned in their coaches' group to help the player think through the problem.

6. Reverse roles for the second problem.

Organizer D: Reciprocal Learning Worksheet for Player A

Player A's Questions	Answers to Player B's Questions and Coaching Hints

Organizer E: Reciprocal Learning Worksheet for Player B

Player B's Questions	Answers to Player A's Questions and Coaching Hints

Collaborative Summarizing

Strategy Overview

Imagine you've just taught a lesson to a sixth-grade class—let's say a lesson on the probability of an event. Now, let's also imagine that over the last few weeks you've been working to develop students' summarizing skills. At the end of the lesson, you ask students to open their math journals and to write a one-paragraph summary of what they've learned. Jared's summary goes like this:

> Probability of an event is the chance that a particular event will happen. It is usually written as a ratio, which is not actually a fraction but can be written in fraction form, like $\frac{2}{9}$. In the probability ratio $\frac{2}{9}$, the 2 represents the number of possible outcomes for a particular event. The 9 represents the total number of possible outcomes. For example, imagine you have a bag with nine pieces of candy. Now let's say that two of the candies are chocolate bars. The probability that you will pull a chocolate bar out of the bag is 2 out of 9, or $\frac{2}{9}$. Probability of an event can be anywhere from 0, which means the event will never happen, to 1, which means the event will always happen.

Based on Jared's summary, how confident would you be that he has a deep understanding of the lesson and is ready to move on to more complex topics?

Jared's writing represents the power of summarizing, and it is the reason that educational researchers like Rick Wormeli (2005) have identified summarizing as one of the most powerful teaching and learning strategies. Students who know how to summarize their learning and new ideas have a significant advantage over students who have a hard time separating the essential from the trivial. After all, how can we expect students to construct new knowledge on top of what they've already learned if they can't call up and restate what they've learned in the first place? What will happen to students who can't summarize the probability of a single event when you move on to the probability of compound events or begin folding in concepts like dependent and independent events?

Obviously, summarizing is important for helping students gain control over content, yet many students lack the skills needed to develop quality summaries. Even worse, many teachers take summarizing skills for granted, assuming that students will simply be able to prioritize and restate concisely what they've learned.

Collaborative Summarizing is a strategy that taps into the power of cooperative learning and "consensus negotiation"—working together to discuss and negotiate the most important ideas in a text or body of content—to help students build their summarizing skills. The strategy also enhances students' ability to analyze summaries and identify the key criteria that separate a high-quality summary from the rest.

How to Use the Strategy

1. Provide students with a reading (or group of short readings) related to the mathematical concepts being studied. (The strategy also works with lectures, demonstrations, and any other form of input that lends itself to summarizing.)

2. Have students read the text on their own and generate a list of what they think are the three to five most important ideas. (For more difficult readings or mathematical concepts, you may have students do their initial reading with a partner.)

3. Organize students into pairs, and review the basic rules for consensus negotiation: Use evidence; avoid snap decisions; be respectful.

4. Have students negotiate their initial lists into the five most important ideas from the reading.

5. Organize student pairs into groups of four.

6. Ask students to renegotiate their two lists into a comprehensive list of the five most important ideas.

7. Have student groups use their lists to organize and prepare a written summary.

8. Allow each group of four students to meet with another group so they can share their summaries with each other.

9. Instruct each group of eight students to develop a set criteria for powerful summaries that they will share with the class and use to write summaries of future readings.

The Strategy in Action

As part of their unit, *People in History . . . Keeping Math Alive*, Michael Sanzo's sixth graders are reading about the history of the calendar year and the mathematical adjustments that have been made to keep the calendar aligned with the solar year. Michael has decided to use Collaborative Summarizing to make sure that all students have a strong grasp on the reading.

Michael begins the lesson by asking students to read the text silently on their own. Once students have read the article for the gist, Michael has them reread it, this time listing what they believe are the five most important ideas. Figure 4.5 shows how two different students—Claire and Kevin—completed their lists.

Kevin's List	Claire's List
1. Earth has two natural units of time: the day and the year.	1. A solar year is not exactly the same as a 365-day calendar year.
2. A true solar year equals 365.242 days.	2. To make a better calendar, the Romans invented the leap year.
3. Because a solar year is not a round number, making an accurate calendar is difficult.	3. Pope Gregory and astronomers took 10 days off the calendar.
4. In 45 BC, Sosigenes invented the leap year to help solve the problem.	4. However, there would still be a small error of about 3 days every 400 years.
5. In 1582, Pope Gregory removed 10 days from the calendar and made years that are multiples of 100 not be leap years unless they were also multiples of 400.	5. Pope Gregory also decided that years that were multiples of 100 would no longer count as leap years.

FIGURE 4.5   Kevin's and Claire's Lists

Next, Michael has students pair up, and he reviews the rules for consensus negotiation with students:

- Be respectful of your partner's ideas.
- Think about why each idea may or may not be particularly important—avoid snap judgments.
- Use evidence from the text to explain your reasons for selecting your ideas.

Using these rules to guide them, Kevin and Claire negotiate their ideas and synthesize their list as follows.

1. A true solar year equals 365.242 days.

2. This creates a problem for calendar makers.

3. The first person to try to solve this was the Roman astronomer Sosigenes, who added one extra day every four years.

4. By 1582, the calendar was off by 11 days, so Pope Gregory advanced the calendar and skipped ahead 10 days.

5. Pope Gregory also canceled leap years that were multiples of 100, except for years that were multiples of 400.

Student pairs then meet up with other pairs to share their lists and compile a final list that all four members can agree on. For this final list, Michael instructs group members to try to get their lists into an order that makes sense, so they will have an easier time converting their lists into a written summary. Together, Claire, Kevin, Paola, and Chase negotiate this final list:

1. A true solar year equals 365.242 days, not 365 days.

2. Julius Caesar's astronomer, Sosigenes, created the leap year, which added one day to the calendar every four years.

3. In 1582, Pope Gregory removed 10 days from the calendar.

4. They realized that the calendar would still be off by about three days every 400 years.

5. Pope Gregory declared multiples of 100 would no longer be leap years unless the year was also a multiple of 400.

The groups of four then work together to create a concise summary of the reading:

> Throughout history, people have needed to adjust their calendars because of the difference between the actual time it takes the earth to revolve around the sun, 365.242 days, and the 365-day calendar. To make their calendars work, the Romans created a leap year and added one extra day, February 29th, to every fourth year. This still did not solve the problem because by 1582 the calendar year was off by 11 days. Pope Gregory adjusted the calendar by removing 10 days and decreeing that years that are multiples of 100 would no longer be leap years. But there was an exception to this rule. Since there would still be a difference of about 3 days every 400 years, years that were also multiples of 400 would remain leap years. Even with all of the adjustments, there is still a very small difference between our calendar year and the earth's rotation around the sun.

For the final phase of the lesson, Michael has each group of four meet with another group to share their summaries with each other and to develop a set of criteria for developing future summaries.

Why the Strategy Works

Summarizing is one of the most important skills any learner can develop. Research shows that students who know how to distill information achieve at higher levels than students who are not able to separate the important from the trivial (Marzano, 2007). Some studies (Crismore, 1985; Hattie, Biggs, & Purdie, 1996; Raphael & Kirschner, 1985) show that teaching students how to condense information into a concise summary can lead to student percentile gains of over 30 points.

Collaborative Summarizing helps students build this critical skill by providing three supports:

1. It allows them to capitalize on the benefits of cooperative learning. The group structure of the strategy gives students the opportunity to learn from each other, test and refine the quality of their ideas, and collaborate on their summaries.

2. It teaches them a model for thinking through and prioritizing their ideas. Deciding what's important and what can be cut is the most challenging part of the summarizing process. Collaborative Summarizing includes a set of simple rules for consensus negotiation that forces students to think through and justify the choices they make.

3. It makes room and time for analysis and generalization. Once students have written and shared their summaries, they work together to examine their work, identify its essential features, and then develop a set of criteria for writing quality summaries. These criteria can become the basis for serious classroom discussion as well as guidelines for future summaries.

Planning Considerations

When designing a Collaborative Summarizing lesson, keep the following questions in mind:

1. What will the input be? In other words, what will students be summarizing? A reading? A set of readings? A lecture? A complex problem or situation? Something else?

2. How much help and direction will students need? If students are new to the strategy, you'll need to explain how it works and what's expected of them. You may also want to set aside time for modeling, showing students how you select critical information from a reading. Finally, if students are new to the strategy, you'll need to review and explain the rules for consensus negotiation.

3. What will your role be while students work? Most teachers choose to walk around the room while groups develop their lists, summaries, and criteria. This allows you to observe both individual and group functioning and to step in and serve as a coach when needed.

4. How will students use the criteria they develop? Often, teachers will survey the class and collect all the criteria. Then, you can work with the class to identify similar criteria and guide them to a final set of criteria that they can use again and again. Ask students to keep these criteria in their notebooks or journals for future use. It is also a good idea to create and post a classroom poster that lists the criteria.

Game Competition

Strategy Overview

Students need opportunities to rehearse and refine their understanding of key content and to practice and refine their skills before their knowledge and skills are subject to a grade. But when these opportunities to practice and review amount to little more than worksheets and drills, many students lose motivation. As a result, their learning and their grades often suffer.

One of the best solutions to this common problem is the Game Competition strategy. The Game Competition strategy builds interest, excitement, and fun into the process while providing the repetition, feedback, and opportunity to learn from mistakes that students need to raise their performance levels.

How to Use the Strategy

To implement the Game Competition strategy in your classroom, follow these seven steps:

1. Determine the mathematical content you will focus on or skill you want your students to master.

2. Choose a specific game structure that aligns with the skill or content you are addressing. Game structures included in this section and the skills and content they emphasize are listed below.
   - Algebra War Games (math facts and whole number operations)
   - Integer War Games (adding and subtracting integers)
   - Solve It Fast! (solving two-step equations)
   - What's My Line? (key mathematical concepts and vocabulary)
   - Relay Races (generic)
   - Boggle (generic)

3. Designate team or game leaders who will help to distribute game materials and collect them at the end of the game.

4. Review the rules of the game with your students.

5. Before the students play the game, preview the mathematics students will be using in the game. Demonstrate to the class how the game is actually played.

6. Engage students in the game. Circulate through the classroom to observe and to provide support as needed.

7. Be prepared to stop the class, get the class's attention, and capitalize on important teachable moments.

The Strategy in Action

There are many well-known classroom game formats such as Jeopardy!, Vocabulary Baseball, and Teams-Games-Tournaments (DeVries, Edwards, & Slavin, 1978). There are also wonderful mathematics-based board games such as Magic Gamewerks' *Math Magic* and *Math Magic 2*; Creative Teaching Associates' *Slugger: Sports Math for Grades 5–9*; Wiebe, Carlson, & Associates' *Decisions: A Stock Market Game*; and Dimension 2000's *Fraction Alley*.

Here, we highlight six ready-to-use game formats. The first five of these games were designed or modified by Ed Thomas (2009b) as part of his *High Achievement* math program. The sixth game, Boggle, comes from Silver, Strong, and Perini's (2001) *Tools for Promoting Active, In-Depth Learning*. Each game is explained and broken down into clear procedures so the teacher can successfully apply any of them in his or her math classes.

Algebra War Games

Purpose: Algebra War Games is designed to reinforce students' math facts, strengthen mental math skills, help students understand the concept of variables, and practice evaluating algebraic expressions.

Materials: One deck of 52 playing cards for each pair of students

How the Game Is Played

Each student is assigned a learning partner. Players are identified as Player A and Player B. Each student receives 26 cards from the shuffled deck. Aces = 1, face cards = 10, and all other cards equal the numbers printed on the cards. Prior to the start of the game, the teacher will use the variable x to represent the value of Player A's first card, and the variable y to represent the value of Player B's card. The teacher will also create a winning game rule by writing an algebraic expression in terms of x and y. For example, the teacher might say that the winning game rule is $2x + y$.

Upon Player A's command, "Go!" each player will place a card face up on the desk or table. If Player A's card has value 8 and Player B's card has value 5, then $x = 8$ and $y = 5$. Because the winning game rule is $2x + y$, the first player to say the answer 21 ($2 \bullet 8 + 5 = 21$) wins the two cards. Upon the next command, "Go!" by Player A, two more cards will be placed on the desk or table. If Player A's card is an ace and Player B's card is a jack then $x = 1$ and $y = 10$. Since the winning game rule is $2x + y$, the first player to say the answer 12 ($2 \bullet 1 + 10 = 12$) wins the two cards. If both players say the answer at the same time (tie), the two cards are moved to the side.

Player A says, "Go!" and two more cards are placed on the table. The first player to say the correct answer wins those two cards plus the two cards from the tie. After a few minutes, the teacher will change the winning game rule and write a new algebraic expression on the board. Popular game rules for the Algebra War Game are: $x + y$; xy; $x - y$; $x^2 + 1$; $xy + 1$; $(x - y)^2$; and $(x + y)^2$.

Extensions of Algebra War Games

1. Students can play in groups of three. For three students, introduce the variable z, and work it into the winning algebraic expression.

2. Once students understand the game, they can be invited to create their own winning game rules.

3. After the game has been played for a while, students who win can be paired together. The runners up can be paired together as well. This allows for better competition.

Integer War Games

Purpose: Integer War Games is designed to reinforce students' ability to combine, add, and subtract positive and negative numbers.

Materials: One deck of 52 playing cards for each pair of students

How the Game Is Played

Integer War Games works like Algebra War Games, except that hearts and diamonds represent negative values. (Black aces = 1, black face cards = 10, and all other black cards equal the numbers printed on the cards. Red aces = –1, red face cards = –10, and all other red cards equal the negative value of the numbers printed on the cards.) Similar to Algebra War Games, the teacher uses the variable x to represent the value of Player A's first card, and the variable y to represent the value of Player B's card. The teacher also creates a winning game rule by writing the algebraic expression $x + y$ on the board.

Upon Player A's command, "Go!" each player will place a card face up on the desk or table. If Player A's card has value –9 and Player B's card has value –3 then $x = -9$ and $y = -3$. Since the winning game rule is $x + y$, the first player to say the answer –12 ($-9 + -3 = -12$) wins the two cards. Once again, if both players say the answer at the same time (tie), the two cards are moved to the side, two more cards are placed on the table, and the first player to say the correct answer wins those two cards plus the two cards from the tie. Every few minutes, the teacher changes the winning game rule. Popular rules are: $x + y$; xy; $x - y$; $x^2 + 1$; and $xy + 1$.

Extensions of Integer War Games

Students can play in groups of three. For three students, introduce the variable z, and work it into the game-winning algebraic expression. For example, $2x + y - z$.

Solve It Fast!

Purpose: Solve It Fast! is designed to help students understand and become proficient in solving algebraic equations.

Materials: One deck of 52 playing cards for each pair of students; one teacher-made Solve It Fast! game board (A Solve It Fast! game board is shown in Figure 4.6.)

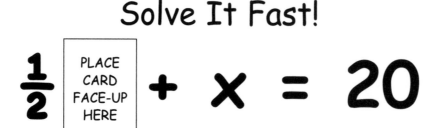

Solve It Fast!

$$\frac{1}{2} \boxed{\text{PLACE CARD FACE-UP HERE}} + x = 20$$

On the command "*Go!*" place your card on the rectangle.
Be the first to solve for *x* by inspection!

FIGURE 4.6   Sample Solve It Fast! Game Board

How the Game Is Played

Similar to the previous two games, each student is assigned a learning partner. Players are identified as Player A and Player B. Each student receives 26 cards from the shuffled deck. Aces = 1, face cards = 10, and all other cards equal the numbers printed on the cards. Prior to the start of the game, the teacher will teach or review with students how to solve an equation by inspection. For example, in the equation $4x + 5 = 29$, students need to ask themselves, "What number + 5 = 29?" and "What number times 4 = 24?"

On Player A's command, "Go!" Player A will place a card face up on the rectangle on the Solve It Fast! game board. The first player to say the correct value of x that makes the equation true wins the card. Throughout the game, Players A and B alternate placing the card on the game board. At the end of the game, the player with the most cards wins the game.

Extensions of Solve It Fast!

1. Different game boards can be made to incorporate fractions, decimals, and even square and cube roots into the game.

2. Solve It Fast! can be played with red cards representing negative values and black cards representing positive values.

What's My Line?

Purpose: What's My Line? is a geometry game that was adapted from the classic *What's My Line?* television show. The purpose of the geometry version is to engage students in critical thinking and deductive reasoning as they listen carefully to clues, make and test conjectures, and work to figure out key mathematical terms and concepts.

How the Game Is Played

In the 1950s and 1960s, John Charles Daly moderated a popular television game show called *What's My Line?* (Alter, Satenstein, Goodson, & Todman, 1950–1967). On the show, a panel of four celebrities was challenged to guess the occupation of a guest contestant. The guest usually had an interesting and important occupation. One at a time, the panel members would ask the guest a yes-or-no question. After hearing the question, the guest would truthfully answer yes or no. Each time a panelist received an answer yes, he or she could ask another question. An answer of no ended the panelist's turn, and the next panelist would then ask a question. Members of the panel would try to ask thoughtful questions whose answers would quickly lead them to pinpoint the contestant's occupation. The first panelist who correctly guessed the occupation won the round. The contestant won the round after giving ten honest no answers.

To adapt the popular format of the classic game show to mathematical concepts, follow these six steps:

1. Explain that you are going to play the game with the class. Instead of a guest with an occupation, the teacher will challenge the class with a mystery term or expression from the unit. (See Figure 4.7 for a sample topic and questions.)

2. All students in the class will serve as the panel, but only students who raise their hand and are selected may ask yes-or-no questions.

3. If the question results in a yes answer, the student can ask another question. If the question results in a no answer, the student's turn is ended, and the teacher will select another student to ask a question.

4. The class's goal is to guess the mystery term or expression before the 10th no answer. After the 10th no answer, the teacher declares that he or she has stumped the class and has won the challenge. If the class guesses the mystery term before the 10th no answer, then the class wins.

5. If the class wins, you may choose to reward students with a small prize.

6. Play What's My Line? at strategic times to optimize student interest and success. For example, a teacher might schedule the game 5 minutes before the end of class as an *out the door* activity.

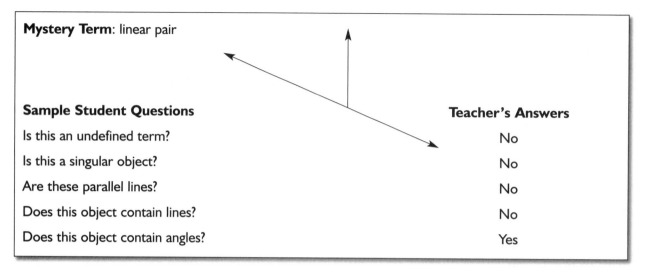

Mystery Term: linear pair

Sample Student Questions   **Teacher's Answers**

Is this an undefined term?   No

Is this a singular object?   No

Are these parallel lines?   No

Does this object contain lines?   No

Does this object contain angles?   Yes

FIGURE 4.7   Sample What's My Line? Questions for *Linear Pair*

Extensions of What's My Line?

1. Students can be invited to select their own mystery term and play the role of game moderator for the class.

2. In addition to mathematical concepts and vocabulary, What's My Line? can be applied to famous numbers or mathematicians.

Relay Races

Purpose: This game is designed to provide students with quality practice and immediate feedback on their work. The class will be divided into four or five teams. Members from each team will compete at the white board or chalkboard. Competition will center on problems for students to solve. Teams will be awarded points for finishing first and for correct answers.

Materials: Whiteboard or chalkboard with writing instruments

How the Game Is Played

To implement Relay Races, follow the 11 steps below.

1. Select a skill that students need to practice.

2. Divide the class into teams (usually four or five) and assign the numbers 1, 2, 3 . . . to the members of each team. After numbers are assigned, each team should have a Player 1, Player 2, and so on.

3. At the board, create a workspace for each team and a team score table.

4. Call Player 1 from each team to the board. Ask these current competitors to face the back of the room.

5. While they look away, write a problem to solve at the top and center of the board. Go to the back of the room, face the competitors, and say, "Go!"

6. Upon the command, "Go!" the competitors will quickly turn and solve the problem, showing their work in their team's space.

7. Instruct students to circle their answer, put their writing tool down, and return to their seats as soon as they complete the problem.

8. Take note of the first finisher, and put a star on that team's workspace.

9. After all the competitors complete their work, go to the board and review with the class how to work through the problem.

10. Assign points to the teams, one point for each correct answer, plus one point for finishing first with the right answer. Record team points on the team score table.

11. Repeat steps 4 through 10 for all team members.

Extensions for Relay Races

1. Experiment with having all students work through the problem at their seats while the competitors work at the board.

2. When the game reaches the midpoint of completion, you may choose to double the points awarded for correct answers and finishing first.

3. When time does not permit every student to go to the board, randomly select the competitors.

Boggle

Purpose: Boggle is a fun and effective way to help students rehearse and remember information before a quiz, test, or other assessment task. Boggle relies on a dynamic of cooperation and competition that maximizes student engagement. Students review first on their own, then they shore up gaps in their knowledge with a study team. Finally, students compete with members from other study teams to earn points for their study team.

Materials: A Boggle game sheet with space to record

- What the student remembered about the lesson or unit;
- The additional information gathered during group rehearsal;
- Missed information during competition; and
- Total points earned.

How the Game Is Played

1. Ask students to review their notes on previously learned content for 2 minutes.

2. Have students record as many big ideas and important details as they can on their game sheets.

3. Create three- to four-member study teams. Members of the study team have 2 minutes to share their lists and record missing information on their game sheets.

4. Pair up students from different study groups to compete against each other. Students compete for two minutes, earning a point for every idea or key detail they have on their game sheet that their partner doesn't have.

5. Have students return to their team and compute the team's score.

6. Lead a review with the entire class. Identify items that earned students points, and clarify how specific information will be used on the test or quiz.

Extensions for Boggle

To help students focus on the pertinent information and generate and organize their ideas, you may want to provide them with categories to guide their information retrieval.

Why the Strategy Works

Games make for good classroom practice for four big reasons:

1. Games are engaging. As Good and Brophy (2003) explain, "The opportunity to compete can add excitement to classroom activities, whether the competition is for prizes or merely for the satisfaction of winning" (p. 227). It's important to remember, however, that classroom competition must be mild and friendly if it is to be effective. Indeed, research shows that intense competition often leads to embarrassment and dejection on the part of losing students. Be sure to explain the rules of conduct and sportsmanship during classroom games. Discourage a winner-takes-all mentality, and instead focus students' attention on the opportunity to close their books, put down their pencils, and have a little fun.

2. Games reinforce academic learning. Repetition is essential to the retention of information and the development of skills (Jensen, 2005). Games provide students with a chance to practice and rehearse their learning without significant consequences and in a way that's far more motivating than completing worksheets or review exercises independently.

3. Games provide the teacher and student with good formative-assessment information. Games help students and their teacher determine how much and how well students have learned the key content and skills of the unit. What's more, games offer teachers the opportunity to provide real-time feedback to students, so they can increase their chances of success and fine-tune their learning in relatively short order.

4. Games enhance the social environment of the classroom. As long as you keep the emphasis squarely on having fun, games promote social interaction as much as they promote competition.

Planning Considerations

While preparing to implement the Game Competition strategy, keep the following tips in mind:

1. Take time to preview the math students will need to do or know to succeed in the game. The purpose of the Game Competition strategy is to help students master math skills and content. Students should enter the math game with a general knowledge of the math skills and content that will be featured in the game.

2. Be sure to develop and explain the rules of the game and the rules of conduct during the game. Similar to sports, rules and penalties for not following the rules may be needed to maintain a climate where learning can take place.

3. Provide small rewards for students who win. Fun-size candy bars, extra points, and 10 minutes of free time are examples of good rewards for winners.

4. Offer various levels of difficulty, so students can play the games on their level.

5. Consider offering recognition and rewards for improvement and attitude as well as for winning, as a way to minimize a winner-takes-all mentality in the classroom and to allow all students to experience success.

Paired Learner & Cooperative Learning

Strategy Overview

Being in a math class where new concepts are taught almost every day can be a stressful and scary experience for many students. It's easy to forget that math concepts and algorithms that are second nature to teachers are often confusing to students who are experiencing them for the very first time. Students experience even more difficulty when they have to learn alone with minimal support from the teacher. This situation is often compounded when curricular demands and class sizes increase.

So, how can a caring teacher provide comforting support to 25 or more students? The Paired Learner model enables teachers to design engaging learning activities that encourage students to work in pairs, so they can support each other in the learning process. The learning activity includes specific guidelines and roles for both students in the learning pair to maximize engagement, ensure order, and promote deeper learning.

(*Note:* Suggestions for converting Paired Learner lessons into Cooperative Learning lessons that involve three or four students are discussed in the "Variations and Extensions" section of this strategy.)

How to Use the Strategy

To implement the Paired Learner strategy in your classroom, follow the steps below.

1. Explain the purpose of the lesson to students. Is the goal to have your students:

   - Acquire new knowledge (vocabulary, facts, and formulas)?
   - Develop and deepen understanding of math concepts?
   - Become more proficient with important math skills?
   - Experience relevant applications and improve their problem-solving skills?
   - Strengthen their retention of mathematics?

2. Explain the Paired Learner activity format. Here are some options:
   - Daily warm-up
   - Word scramble
   - Proceduralization
   - Modeling and Experimentation
   - Open-ended problem solving

3. Present the activity or problem to students. The activity should be one that encourages communication and collaboration.

4. Make sure students have the tools they need to succeed (visual organizer, rulers, manipulatives, access to electronic or print resources, etc.).

5. Assign partners, preview the mathematics, and explain students' roles before the actual Paired Learner activity.

6. Implement the Paired Learner activity. Circulate around the classroom to provide support to struggling students and partnerships.

7. Synthesize the learning through discussion, a synthesis task, or both.

The Strategy in Action

One of the easiest and most effective ways to use Paired Learner is with application problems that ask students to put the mathematics they've learned into practice while reinforcing key content and skills. For example, during a unit on probability, you might design a Paired Learner activity that looks like Figure 4.8 on page 152.

Here are three other ways to use the Paired Learner model:

Paired Learner: Example 1, Daily Warm-Up

To get the most out of her daily math warm-up, Martina Moran implements the Paired Learner model. Working in pairs, students tackle the daily warm-up problem by

1. Writing the problem on a warm-up record sheet in their math journals;

2. Individually reading the problem, determining what they're being asked to find, and creating a simple sketch or description of the problem solving process;

3. Sharing their findings from step two with their partners and reaching consensus on *what* (what's the problem asking?) and *how* (how should it be solved?);

4. Solving the problem individually; and

5. Working with a partner to check solutions, correct their work, and prepare to share their results with the class.

A sample daily warm-up problem from Dimension 2000's *High Achievement* math program (Thomas, 2009a) for seventh grade is shown in Figure 4.9 on page 153.

Paired Learner: Example 2, Word Scramble

Troy Ballis works hard to keep his math students actively engaged in his classroom. Today, he is using a word-scramble activity to help his

Directions: Work with a learning partner. Open one pack of your favorite colored candies. Count the number of candies for each color represented in the pack. Record your data in the table below. Repeat the experiment for a second pack of the same kind of colored candies.

Colors	Number in First Pack	Number in Second Pack	Average
Red			
Green			
Pink			
Yellow			
Orange			
Blue			
Total			

Create a bar graph that is representative of the average distribution of the colors in the packs of candies. The colors of the bars should correspond to the colors of the candies.

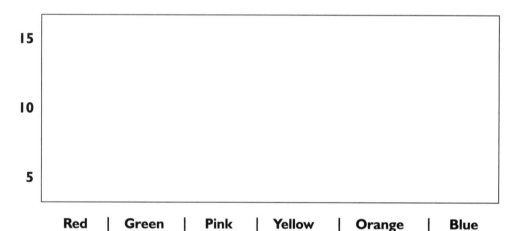

Using your data, approximate the probability of selecting a candy of each color if the candy is randomly drawn from a typical pack. Use the formula:

$$P \text{ (color)} = \frac{\text{average \# of candies of that color}}{\text{average \# of candies in one pack}}$$

FIGURE 4.8   Paired Learner Activity for a Unit on Probability

---

Dr. Thomas's Math Challenge # 41

Triangle ABC has coordinates A(0,0), B(6,0), and C(3,6). Triangle ABC is translated 5 units in the positive direction of the x-axis and reflected across the x-axis. Find the coordinates of the resulting image.

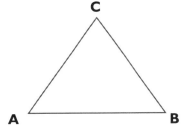

A) (5,–5), (11, –11), (8,–6)
B) (5,0), (11, 0), (8,–6)
C) (–5,0), (–11,0), (–8,6)
D) (–5,5), (–11,11), (–8,6)

1. Find 120% of 50   2. Find $\frac{1}{2}$ of 24   3. $\frac{1}{6} \cdot \frac{1}{9}$

FIGURE 4.9 Sample Daily Warm-Up Problem

students review content and practice a variety of skills in a way that is fun and compelling. Troy's word scramble, shown in Figure 4.10, contains eight problems whose answers correlate with key letters of the alphabet. The key letters represent the scrambled letters of an important math vocabulary word. The students' challenge is to solve the problems correctly, collect the letters, and discover the math word.

For this activity, Troy uses the Paired Learner model as follows.

1. Each student is assigned a learning partner.

2. Individually, each student solves all eight problems.

3. Together, paired learners check each other's answers, discuss differences, and make sure that they have the correct answers.

4. Individually, students collect the key letters that represent the scrambled math word.

5. Together, students work to discover the math word.

Paired Learner: Example 3, Building a House for Pythagoras

Peter Levison has decided to develop a Paired Learner activity that teaches his students the story of Pythagoras and fundamental concepts associated with the Pythagorean theorem. The Paired Learner activity will work as follows.

Directions: The answers to the problems below correspond to letters of the alphabet. These letters are the scrambled form of a common math word. Find the answers and their corresponding letters (use the alphabet chart to find the corresponding letters). Find the math word, and write it at the bottom of the form.

Solution	Letter	
1. _____	_____	$x^0, x \neq 0$
2. _____	_____	How many prime numbers are even?
3. _____	_____	$3\frac{1}{4} + 2\frac{1}{2} + 3\frac{1}{4}$
4. _____	_____	How many edges does a cube have?
5. _____	_____	How many sides does a heptagon have?
6. _____	_____	How many lines of symmetry does a square have?
7. _____	_____	Evaluate $a^2 + 2b - 3c$ for $a = 5$, $b = \frac{1}{2}$, and $c = 4$.
8. _____	_____	Find six less than half the sum of the whole-number factors of 20.

a	1	j	10	s	19	**Math Word:**
b	2	k	11	t	20	
c	3	l	12	u	21	
d	4	m	13	v	22	
e	5	n	14	w	23	
f	6	o	15	x	24	
g	7	p	16	y	25	
h	8	q	17	z	26	
i	9	r	18			

FIGURE 4.10   Troy's Word Scramble

Part I: The Story of Pythagoras

Peter provides each pair of students with two different websites that tell the story of Pythagoras in slightly different ways. The students are instructed to visit their respective websites, read the story, and take notes, so they can tell their version of the story to each other. As students share their stories and information with their partners, they modify their own notes and work together to reach consensus to get their story right.

Part II: Designing a Floor Plan for Pythagoras

Peter challenges each learning pair to design a modern house for Pythagoras. In this phase of the activity, the students' task is to design the floor plan of the house. The floor plan must meet the following standards:

- All rooms must be right triangles.
- The size of the living area must be as close to 3,140 square feet as possible.

- The home must include the following rooms: one master bedroom, two additional bedrooms, two bathrooms, one living room, one dining room, one great room with fireplace, one kitchen, one pantry, one foyer, one den/office, one exercise/recreation room, and one laundry room.
- The dimensions of each room must satisfy the Pythagorean theorem: $a^2 + b^2 = c^2$.

For this task, students in each learning pair share ideas, evaluate each other's ideas, investigate new ideas, and work to reach consensus as they identify and solve problems that arise in the process of designing their floor plan.

Part III: Designing the Exterior of Pythagoras's Home

Next, Peter challenges each learning pair to design the exterior face of Pythagoras's modern house. The main features of the exterior design must include (you guessed it) right triangles. Features of the exterior design can include exterior walls, roof, chimney, windows, shutters, porch, lighting, landscaping, and so on.

As in Part II, students need to think and work collaboratively as they share, evaluate, and implement their ideas.

Part IV: Displaying Students' Work

Students display their final story, floor plan with labels and measures, and exterior design on a three-section project board. Both learning partners' names appear at the top of the project board. All completed project boards are displayed in the media center.

Part V: The Gallery Walk

Administrators, teachers, and students from all math classes are invited to visit the media center and review the final projects submitted by the learning pairs.

In addition to learning a great deal about Pythagoras and the Pythagorean theorem, the students enjoy the interactions afforded by the Paired Learner model and remember their experience for a long time.

Why the Strategy Works

Allowing and encouraging students in math class to pair up and work together from time to time presents powerful opportunities for deep learning. In addition to generating more problem-solving power, students who work together in pairs exercise and improve their collaboration and communication skills (Butler, 1999), spend more time on task, and develop more positive attitudes towards subject matter (King-Sears & Bradley, 1995). The research also shows that student partnerships lead to better classroom discussions (Hashey & Connors, 2003) and increased academic intensity without additional instructional time (Fuchs, Fuchs, Mathes, & Simmons, 1997). Despite all of these findings, any partnership can fail if students are simply told to "work together." Make sure that students' roles and expectations are clear, and look for ways to highlight the work of productive partnerships, so that all students get a strong sense of how they can work together to maximum effect.

Planning Considerations

In designing a Paired Learner activity, keep the following tips in mind:

1. Build in procedures that require students to participate together. Paired Learner activities work well when students are asked to do things like:

- Share and compare ideas with each other;
- Coach one another;
- Analyze and check each other's solutions;
- Create problems for each other to solve; and
- Work together to summarize or synthesize new learning or research.

2. Provide students with the tools they need for success. Will students need

- Resources to acquire missing information?
- Visual organizers?
- Rulers, scissors, tape, or other manipulatives?
- A particular placement of tables, chairs, or desks?

3. Preview important vocabulary, formulas, or math procedures students will need for success. Previewing important information helps students prepare for the activity and enables them to support their learning partner.

4. Provide incentives for learning pairs to do their best work.

5. Be prepared to circulate during the Paired Learner activity and provide assistance to students who need it.

6. Have a plan in place for students who complete the task early. Students who finish their task early can start the homework assignment or create similar problems for each other to solve. They can also be invited to coach other learning pairs who need help.

7. Review and reinforce the problem-solving process. When all students complete the problem-solving task, be sure to assess students' work, allow time for students to correct their work, and include an opportunity to try a similar problem, so they can show that they have learned from their mistakes.

Variations and Extensions

Cooperative Learning

Paired Learner is a variation of Cooperative Learning. The main difference, of course, is that Paired Learner consists of two-member partnerships rather than three- or four-member groups. Most Paired Learner activities and lessons can be adapted for larger cooperative groups rather easily. There may be times during a Paired Learner activity when it becomes beneficial to invite two learning pairs to join together to share or combine results or participate in a procedure that requires four students. For example, in a study of averages, each learning pair may be instructed to measure each other's height and find the average of the two heights. As an extension, two learning pairs might come together and find the average of their averages. Student groups might be asked to determine which of the three measures of central tendency would be most representative of the actual class average.

In addition, Cooperative Learning allows you to engage students in more complex activities and projects. For example, you might design a Cooperative Learning task or lesson that asks students to conduct research or engage in experimental inquiry and problem solving (see Figure 4.11).

Research Project: Home Economics and Math	**Experimental Problem Solving:** The Strongest Paper Tube
In a team of three, conduct an analysis of five different brands of paper towels. Then, develop a system to compare them for different purchasing priorities (durability, softness, cost). Compare your system to the information offered by the brands you chose and consumer reports. Construct graphs to show your results, and use the graphs to form a conclusion. *Assessment Criteria:* • Use of criteria • Research • Analysis • Conclusions • Clarity/quality of graphic information • Conclusions	How much weight can a paper tube really support? In a team of four, test the strength of different paper tubes. Each paper tube must span an open space of six inches, but your team controls the thickness, length, and circumference of each tube you test. Your team will have paper, scissors, glue, tape, string, paper cups, and weight sets to conduct your experiments. As you test your team's paper tubes, record your findings and questions on your own Essential Question Notes organizer. As a final challenge, you must create a paper tube that will hold the greatest amount of weight possible. Your team's design will be tested against designs from other student teams to see which paper tube can hold the most weight. ***Adapted from:*** Silver, H. F., Brunsting, J. R., & Walsh, T. (2008). *Math Tools, Grades 3-12: 64 Ways to Differentiate Instruction and Increase Student Engagement.* (p. 256)

FIGURE 4.11   Two Cooperative Learning Activities

While cooperative learning is one of the best-researched and most-effective classroom practices, most teachers have experienced Cooperative Learning lessons that have failed to meet expectations. Many of these failures can be attributed, not to problems inherent in cooperative learning, but rather to the lack of distinction between a true Cooperative Learning activity and mere group work. When teachers place students into groups and hope for the best, the results will almost always be disappointing. As David and Roger Johnson (1999), two of the leading experts on Cooperative Learning in the classroom, point out, successful Cooperative Learning activities are designed around five principles of success:

1. Interdependence. Emphasize that members are linked and that they need to rely on each other—not only themselves—if they expect to succeed. Other ways to increase students' sense of interdependence include the use of a grading system that rewards contributions to the group and placing a spotlight on groups that are working effectively.

2. Individual accountability. To make sure there is no divide between "loafers" and conscientious students, walk around the room to observe individual effort. You may also choose to have group members assess each other's efforts individually and confidentially.

3. Face-to-face interaction. Model positive face-to-face behaviors like active listening, providing encouragement, and praising effort with students or with other teachers serving as models. Remind students that negative group behaviors, such as hostility and name calling, are unacceptable; circulate and observe while students work.

4. Small group skills. Cooperative Learning works best when groups are small (three or four students) and students know how to work productively with fellow group members. To build students' small group skills, you may want to choose a focus skill, such as conflict resolution, consensus negotiation, or group communication, and design Cooperative Learning lessons so that they highlight it.

5. Group processing. Successful groups think about more than the content they're learning; they also pay attention to the functioning of the group. That's why it's always important to leave time for reflection, self-assessment, and whole-class discussion.

5

Multistyle Strategies

OVERVIEW

Multistyle strategies combine the thinking of all four styles to help students become *complete, multifaceted problem solvers*, who can . . .

- *Use Mastery-style thinking to* remember critical facts and procedures, and apply mathematical conventions;
- *Use Understanding-style thinking to* analyze data and problem-solving situations, and explain mathematical concepts;
- *Use Self-Expressive-style thinking to* solve nonroutine problems and represent mathematical ideas in a variety of ways; and
- *Use Interpersonal-style thinking to* connect the mathematics they're learning to their lives beyond the school walls and work as part of a team to solve problems and discuss mathematical ideas.

The three *Multistyle strategies* in this chapter can help you meet these *NCTM Process Standards.*

Strategy	NCTM Process Standards*				
	Problem Solving	**Reasoning and Proof**	**Communication**	**Connections**	**Representation**
Task Rotation **[p. 161]** Students are given four tasks (one in each style) focused on a topic and complete all four tasks in order or have the choice of which tasks they want to complete.	✓	✓	✓	✓	
Math Notes [p. 171] Students use all four styles of thinking to analyze, visualize, and solve challenging word problems.	✓	✓	✓		✓
Integrated Math Engagement [p. 182] Students solve well-designed problems that require them to apply what they know about concepts and procedures and to investigate how these concepts and procedures are interrelated.	✓	✓	✓	✓	✓

FIGURE 5.0 Correlation of Multistyle Strategies to NCTM Process Standards

*For more information on the National Council of Teachers of Mathematics (NCTM) Process Standards, please consult their *Principles and Standards for School Mathematics* (2000), or visit their website at www.nctm.org.

Task Rotation

Strategy Overview

"All students can learn!" Inspirational words to some; but sadly, that slogan rings hollow in the ears of too many teachers of mathematics—teachers who, in spite of passionate efforts, keep coming to the same two questions:

1. Why do so many students significantly underachieve in mathematics?

2. What can I do to improve mathematics achievement of all my students, not just my academic superstars?

What these concerned teachers keep running up against is the so-called "math crisis," that terrible, haunting idea that the majority of our students simply aren't developing the mathematical skills and knowledge they need to succeed in today's world.

It doesn't have to be this way. In fact, the work of Robert J. Sternberg (2006), Dean of Arts and Sciences at Tufts University and past president of the American Psychological Association, suggests that we can engage all our math students and raise achievement across the board if we pay attention to two little words: *learning styles.* What Sternberg discovered in a series of studies involving students from across the country and the globe is this: when math teachers incorporate a variety of styles into their instructional program, their students routinely do better on both performance assessments *and* objective tests than students who receive "traditional" math instruction.

Task Rotation offers a simple and effective way to differentiate teaching and learning via learning styles. To design a Task Rotation, a teacher develops four separate learning tasks. Each task in Figure 5.1 highlights a specific kind of thinking or learning style:

Mastery	Interpersonal
Mastery tasks ask students to remember facts and demonstrate their proficiency with a procedure or skill.	*Interpersonal tasks* ask students to explore the personal, social, and real-world implications of mathematics.
For example... State the Pythagorean theorem, then draw an appropriate sketch.	**For example...** Identify a job or career in which the Pythagorean theorem might be helpful. Compare your ideas with a partner. Then, work together to develop a job description for one of your jobs that explains why knowing the Pythagorean theorem is a big plus.
Assign values to two sides of your sketch, and find the value of the third side.	

(Continued)

(Continued)

Understanding	Self-Expressive
Understanding tasks ask students to uncover and explain the principles and big ideas behind the math they learn.	*Self-Expressive tasks* ask students to use their imagination and to think creatively to solve nonroutine problems.
For example... Argue for or against this statement: *The Pythagorean theorem can be applied to all triangles.* Explain your answer.	*For example...* Make a scale drawing of a rectangular area that's interesting to you (e.g., a football field, a volleyball court, a sheet cake, a dance floor). Then, create a word problem that incorporates your rectangle and that requires the problem solver to use the Pythagorean theorem to find the answer. (Don't be afraid to be creative!) Solve your problem.

FIGURE 5.1   Pythagorean Theorem Task Rotation

A great benefit of Task Rotation is its flexibility. It can be used in a variety of ways to meet a host of instructional and assessment objectives. For example, you can design Task Rotations that ask students to

- Complete all four tasks in a specific sequence (facilitates deep, layered learning);
- Complete one or two tasks and then choose another (ideal for covering critical material while also offering some choice to students); or
- Freely select the tasks they want to complete (empowers students to make choices and take responsibility for their learning).

How to Use the Strategy

1. If your students are unfamiliar with learning styles, introduce them to the four learning styles, and allow them time for reflection and discussion. Student understanding of learning styles will help them become more aware of their natural problem-solving inclinations and more attuned to what a given problem is asking of them.

2. Introduce the four tasks of the Task Rotation. Make it clear that students are being asked to

- Look at a topic from four distinct angles or task perspectives;
- Be aware of their task preferences and comfort with each; and
- Share, when completed, their discovered relationships between and among the four activity types.

3. Explain student roles. It is very important that students understand what is expected of them and how they are to function. Will students be completing all of the tasks or some of the tasks? Do they have choices as to which tasks to complete? Must the tasks be completed in a particular sequence or is there a choice?

4. Allow students to complete the tasks either alone or with a cooperative-learning group. Provide criteria for success if needed.

5. Observe students while they work and listen to their conversations. Observing students as they select and complete tasks is an ideal way to learn more about each student's preferences and personal approach to learning.

6. Conclude Task Rotations with class opportunities for student reflection and discussion. Encourage students to first think about and then answer questions such as these:

- What kind of mathematical thinking was required by each task?
- Which task was your favorite? Which was your least favorite?
- What did you learn about yourself during the lesson?
- How can you improve yourself as a learner?

The Strategy in Action

Juanita Thompson is nearing the end of a unit on fractions and mixed numbers. Today, she hands out a Task Rotation called Operation Fractions! (Figure 5.2 on page 164) and asks students to review its four tasks.

Juanita tells students that today's Task Rotation will blend some assignment with some free choice. It will also include both individual work and cooperative work. She says, "First, all students will complete the Mastery Task on their own. So, let's look at the Mastery Task and see if we can figure out why it's essential that we complete it."

After surveying students' ideas, Juanita and the class agree that being able to complete the Mastery Task would mean students could handle all the basic operations in the unit and that they could confidently manipulate fractions in their various forms. Students then work on the Mastery Task while Juanita moves around the room to observe students in action and provide assistance to struggling students.

Once students have completed the Mastery Task, they pair up with a learning partner. "What you're going to do now," explains Juanita, "is to check and compare your answers and your work on the Mastery Task. Then, once you and your partner are certain that your work is accurate and correct, you'll work together to choose and complete one of the three remaining tasks. Whichever task you choose, you and your partner should be prepared to present your work to the entire class."

As students discuss and complete their chosen tasks, Juanita overhears many comments about personal preferences. Though she knows her students quite well, Juanita is always awed by the insights into student thinking that Task Rotation lessons offer her. Juanita learns even more

Mastery (Task One)	*Interpersonal (Task Two)*
Use the rules of fractions to perform the following operations. Copy each problem, show your work, and simplify your answers. $3\frac{1}{2} + 2\frac{1}{4}$ $4\frac{1}{4} - 1\frac{1}{4}$ $2\frac{1}{2} \cdot 4\frac{1}{5}$ $4\frac{1}{2} \div 2\frac{1}{4}$	$2\frac{1}{4} + 1\frac{1}{2} = 3\frac{3}{4}$ Show that this equation is true in two different ways. First, use the grid below. Then, show that the same equation is true using our tiles. Which method of representation do you prefer? Which method do you think would make the process clearer for a young student who's learning to add mixed numbers for the first time? 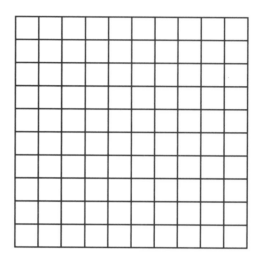
Understanding (Task Three) The algorithm for dividing two fractions is as follows. *To divide two fractions:* 1. *Rewrite the first fraction;* 2. *Invert the second fraction; and* 3. *Multiply both fractions together.* Study this algorithm. On poster paper, copy the algorithm, and explain why the procedure works.	*Self-Expressive (Task Four)* Create a fraction problem—with at least two different operations—that, on the surface, appears to be complex but simplifies to a very simple answer (like 0 or 1). Display your problem *and* its solution for the class.

FIGURE 5.2 Operation Fractions! Task Rotation

about students' perspectives on mathematics and their level of comprehension during the student presentations.

Juanita concludes the lesson with a discussion in which students share their thoughts on

- The kinds of thinking required by each task;
- Which tasks they liked best and which they chose to avoid;

- What their approach to selecting and completing tasks taught them about themselves; and
- How they can capitalize on their natural strengths and minimize areas of weakness.

In another classroom, Cal Sanzone is using Task Rotation with his sixth graders to help them develop their data analysis skills. Unlike Juanita's lesson, Cal has his students complete all the tasks in a prescribed order. He sets up his Task Rotation by creating an engaging hook that is designed to get students to take a more active role in the lesson:

> You are the coach of the Stars basketball team. Your team is one point behind and, at the final buzzer, a two-shot technical foul has been called on your opponent, the Flames. You have to select one of your five players to shoot the two free throws. If the player makes the first free throw, the game goes into overtime. If the player makes both free throws, you win the game. Who would you choose and why?

Next, Cal provides them with the data they will need to complete the Task Rotation (Figure 5.3).

Player	Free Throws During the Season	Free Throws in the Last Two Minutes of the Game
Tanya	12 out of 15	1 out of 3
Elizabeth	40 out of 50	18 out of 27
Mora	45 out of 60	12 out of 16
Shanika	9 out of 18	4 out of 4
Maria	27 out of 54	15 out of 25

FIGURE 5.3 Table of Data for Task Rotation

Then, he gives students the Task Rotation (Figure 5.4) and reviews each task as well as the order of the tasks before having students get to work.

Mastery (First)	*Interpersonal (Third)*
Does the team shoot better during the last 2 minutes than it does during the season?	Who did you choose to shoot the free throw? Why?
What is the overall percentage for the season? For the last 2 minutes?	Did you use any factors other than statistical evidence to make your choice?
What is the difference in percentage between the free throws made during the season vs. the last 2 minutes?	

(Continued)

(Continued)

Understanding (Second)	*Self-Expressive (Fourth)*
As you're making your decision about who should shoot the final free throws, your assistant coach urges you to stop looking at the numbers and to simple go with the "hot hand." Do you agree or disagree with this advice? Explain.	The game is over and your team has won. How did it happen? Write a brief piece for your school newspaper that captures the drama of the last few minutes of the game. Be sure to use the table to incorporate at least four accurate pieces of data (e.g., individual percentages, team percentages, free throws attempted vs. made, etc.).

FIGURE 5.4   Data Analysis Task Rotation

Why the Strategy Works

In the introduction to this book, we discussed briefly the history of learning styles, from their inception in the work of Carl Jung in the early 1920s all the way to their adaptation to the specific demands of the mathematics classroom (Silver, Thomas, & Perini, 2003). This final adaptation led to the mathematical learning-styles model (shown in Figure i.5 in the Introduction), which gives this book its structure.

So, why learning styles? With all the content mathematics teachers need to cover and with all these standards screaming to be addressed, can teachers of mathematics really afford to pay attention to learning styles? The answer, of course, is yes. And a better question is, with so many students struggling in secondary mathematics classrooms—with so many students tuning out, turning away, and falling victim to the "terrors of math anxiety"—how can teachers of mathematics afford not to pay attention to the different ways their students learn? Or, try it this way: Will plowing through more content without addressing the learning needs of students lead to better learning or academic improvement?

Task Rotation is a strategy that makes it relatively easy for teachers of mathematics to reap the significant benefits of style-based instruction. These benefits include

1. Style-based instruction raises student achievement. In a series of studies involving students from all over the world, Robert Sternberg (2006) and his colleagues taught mathematics using five different instructional approaches:

- A memory-based approach emphasizing recall of facts and concepts;
- An analytical approach emphasizing critical thinking and comparative analysis;
- A creative approach emphasizing imagination and invention;
- A practical approach emphasizing the application of concepts to real-world situations; and
- A diverse approach that incorporated all the approaches.

During these studies, two distinct patterns emerged. First, students who were taught through an approach that matched their own learning styles nearly always did better than students who were mismatched. Second, the students who did the best of all were those students who were taught using all of the approaches rather than any single approach. They did better on memory drills, they did better on objective tests, and they did better on performance assessments.

2. Style-based instruction equals good mathematics. A simple scan of the NCTM's *Principles and Standards for School Mathematics* (2000) will remind us of the need to help students see mathematics through multiple lenses that look an awful lot like the four styles:

- Mathematics is . . . following directions, mastering procedures, and calculating correct answers!
- Mathematics is . . . the application of procedures and the understanding of how and why they work!
- Mathematics is . . . purposeful, relevant, and useful in our lives!
- Mathematics is . . . a language, a tool of creativity and self-expression!

3. Task Rotation can help teachers and students of mathematics meet a variety of learning goals. These goals include

- *Increasing depth of understanding*—students' comprehension of new material will be deeper because they regularly examine new content from different perspectives.
- *Improving thinking*—students become more proficient in four distinct styles of thinking: remembering (Mastery), reasoning (Understanding), creating (Self-Expressive), and relating (Interpersonal).
- *Building motivation*—students become more engaged in the learning process because Task Rotation lessons balance work in their own personal style with explorations of new and different approaches to learning.
- *Promoting flexibility*—students' thinking becomes more open and flexible as they work on tasks requiring different ways of thinking and learning.

Planning Considerations

Designing a Task Rotation involves six steps:

1. Collect your standards. Collect the most important standards associated with the topic or concept. Select the standards that address the specific content, skills, and processes your Task Rotation will highlight.

2. Identify your purpose. Given your topic and standards, specify the knowledge, understandings, skills, and attitudes you want students to develop by answering these questions:

- What do you want students to *know*?
- What do you want students to *understand*?

- What *skills* do you want students to *demonstrate?*
- What *connections* do you want students to make?

For example, a Task Rotation on the topic of percentages might be built upon the following knowledge, understandings, skills, and connections:

- Students will *know* the process for converting a fraction to percentage;
- Students will *understand* the relationship between fractions and percentages, including how fractions and percentages are similar and different;
- Students will be able to represent a specific percentage (e.g., 40%) in at least five different ways (*skills*); and
- Students will use percentages to describe aspects of life at home, at school, or at play (*personal connections*).

3. Design a task in each of the four learning styles. Use the knowledge, understanding, skills, and personal connections you identified to guide the design of your four tasks. For example, the previous Task Rotation on data analysis (see Figure 5.4, pages 165–166) is designed around the sample learning goals—know, understand, skills, and personal connections—presented in Step 2 above.

4. Create a "hook" to capture students' interest and activate prior knowledge. Student attention is a requirement for deep learning. When developing a Task Rotation, look for an attention-grabbing hook. A hook is a question or activity designed to capture student interest. For example, take a second look at how Cal Sanzone introduced his data-analysis Task Rotation (Figure 5.4) in "The Strategy in Action" section.

5. Develop criteria for success. For each of the tasks, develop criteria consistent with your purposes. For example, the sixth-grade teacher who developed the percentages Task Rotation designed the following criteria for the four tasks:

- Do students know the process that converts a fraction into an equivalent percentage?
- Are students able to put into words the similarities and differences between fractions and percentages?
- Are students able to develop creative, nonverbal representations of common percentages?
- Are students able to identify and describe personal connections to percentages?
- Take time to clearly describe to students the criteria so that they understand what quality work entails.

6. Establish a work plan. The flexibility of Task Rotation provides the teacher with many options for instruction and assessment. A Task Rotation work plan will specify whether the student will work individually, in pairs, in groups, or some combination of the three. It will also specify whether students will

- Complete all tasks in a required sequence;
- Complete all tasks in a sequence of their choosing;
- Complete one or two assigned tasks and one or two of their choosing; or
- Complete one or two tasks of their choosing.

Whatever you decide, remember that a Task Rotation provides you with a unique opportunity to observe students making learning choices and operating in their preferred styles as well as their weaker styles. Its value as a formative-assessment tool cannot be overstated.

Variations and Extensions

Learning Styles and the "Eight Cs of Student Engagement"

Student engagement is critical to learning in any classroom, and a great deal of research has been conducted over the last few years on the mysteries and benefits of student engagement. In summarizing the results from over 75 studies on engagement in the classroom, Robert Marzano (2007) concludes, "Arguably, keeping students engaged is one of the most important considerations for the classroom teacher" (p. 98).

In their recent work investigating the links between learning styles and student engagement, Harvey Silver and Matthew Perini (2009) identified a "set of reliable motivators" that teachers could use to engage all four learning styles. They called these motivators the "Eight Cs of Student Engagement." In Figure 5.5, we show how mathematics teachers can use these eight Cs to increase engagement in the classroom.

The Eight Cs	Description	Examples
Competition	Friendly competition! Students are often energized in the classroom by an element of competition. Give students time and incentive to learn and review through friendly but competitive games.	Use the gaming structures from Game Competition (pages 141–149) to help students shore up gaps in their comprehension and prepare for tests.
Challenge	Many students like a challenge! Encourage them to strive for excellence.	Use Graduated Difficulty (pages 36–41) and Graduated Warm-Ups that encourage students to select tasks at the right level of challenge.
Curiosity	Pique students' natural curiosity by presenting mathematics as a mystery to be solved.	• Yes, $5^0 = 1$, but why? • Math riddles: "I am a three-digit number. All of my digits . . ." • "Did you ever wonder how people did division and multiplication using Roman numerals? Let's find out."

(Continued)

(Continued)

The Eight Cs	Description	Examples
Controversy	Mathematics is filled with controversies past and present. Allow students to explore controversies and to develop positions.	• Is algebra a discovery or an invention? • Are triangles real? • Why do mathematicians "go crazy" for π?
Cooperation	Encourage students to learn mathematics with others—as part of a community of problem solvers.	Use strategies like Reciprocal Learning (pages 125–135), Collaborative Summarizing (pages 136–140), and Paired Learner (pages 150–158) to get the most out of teams and partnerships.
Connections	Mathematics is everywhere. Let students look for connections between the mathematics they're learning and the world they live in.	• "The assignment for Monday is to find and record at least ten examples of *rates* referenced in newspapers." • Can you think of three ways negative numbers are used in the real world? • Why is it important to know how to calculate area and perimeter?
Choice	Make the most of this natural motivator by letting students select the tasks they wish to complete.	Use Task Rotations, or take choice a step further with Assessment Menus: At the beginning of a unit, provide students with an Assessment Menu of tasks involving three representation forms—algebraic, graphic, and numeric—across all four styles. A total of 12 tasks are offered, and, over the course of the unit, the student must choose four of 12 problems—one in each style and at least one of each of the representation forms.
Creativity	Give students an opportunity to express their own unique ideas as they explore mathematical content.	• Can you find a different way to solve the problem? • Can you create an interesting logo that includes at least two different transformations? • How is factoring like panning for gold?

FIGURE 5.5 The Eight Cs in the Mathematics Classroom

Math Notes

Strategy Overview

Turn on your television any night of the week, and you will probably find a good "problem-solving drama." But what does that mean exactly? Think about wildly popular shows like *House, CSI, Law & Order,* and many other television series that build drama and entertainment from problem solving. Audiences tune in each and every week to follow their favorite characters as they analyze a problem, gather evidence, develop and test hypotheses, and ultimately work towards an elegant or clever solution. Mathematically speaking, problem solving equals one of the most dependable forms of popular entertainment.

In a development of special interest to mathematics teachers, the television show *Numb3rs* (Falacci, Heuton, Scott, & Scott, 2005–present) specifically highlights *mathematical* problem solving. Indeed, each episode of *Numb3rs* applies mathematical problem solving in distinct, discernible steps. *Numb3rs* shows that real problem solving is not a premature rush to an answer but a deliberate, patient process in which a problem solver:

- Collects the facts;
- States the obvious and seeks out the not-so-obvious questions to be answered;
- Diagrams what is known, "picturing" what has or might have happened;
- Plans the logical steps expected to be taken; and
- Works to solve the problem, making adjustments as needed and collaborating whenever possible.

In the classroom, problem-solving opportunities most often appear in the form of *word problems.* As almost any mathematics teacher will tell you, good skills and habits are essential when it comes to solving word problems which, despite their prominence in mathematics textbooks and now on state and national tests, still prove one of the most difficult and frustrating types of problems for most students. Unlike other mathematics problems, word problems require careful reading, interpretation, inference, and the formulation of a plan. If students lack good problem-solving habits, they're susceptible to impulse, to leaping to a first solution without thinking the problem through.

Enter Math Notes. Math Notes is a research-based problem-solving process that focuses and slows down student thinking. Teachers use Math Notes to show students how to systematically work through just about any mathematical problem by selecting and interpreting information, planning, and finding a solution.

To see how Math Notes works, let's first look at a typical middle school word problem:

From a solitary elm tree in an open field, twelve-year-old Ella first walked 50 feet north, then 30 feet east, and finally 10 feet south, where she stopped at an oak tree. Looking back at the elm tree, Ella then walked directly back to it. How much farther was her walk from the elm tree to the oak tree than her return walk directly back to the elm tree?

Using a Math Notes organizer, a student would collect the facts, identify the question, draw a diagram, plan the steps, and finally solve the problem as shown in Figure 5.6.

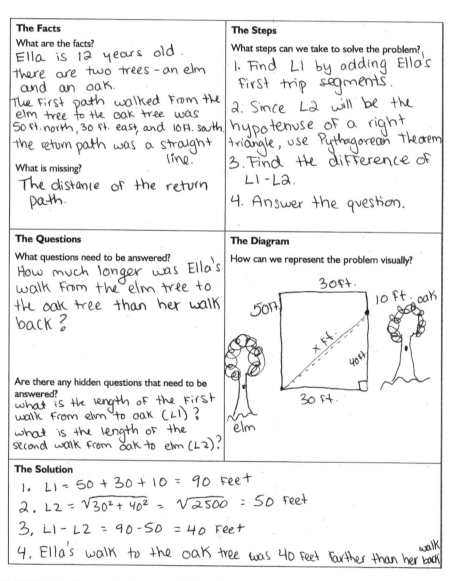

The Facts

What are the facts?
Ella is 12 years old.
there are two trees - an elm and an oak.
The first path walked from the elm tree to the oak tree was 50 ft. north, 30 ft. east, and 10 ft. south. the return path was a straight line.

What is missing?
The distance of the return path.

The Steps

What steps can we take to solve the problem?
1. Find L1 by adding Ella's first trip segments.
2. Since L2 will be the hypotenuse of a right triangle, use Pythagorean theorem
3. Find the difference of L1 - L2.
4. Answer the question.

The Questions

What questions need to be answered?
How much longer was Ella's walk from the elm tree to the oak tree than her walk back?

Are there any hidden questions that need to be answered?
what is the length of the first walk from elm to oak (L1)?
what is the length of the second walk from oak to elm (L2)?

The Diagram

How can we represent the problem visually?

The Solution
1. L1 = 50 + 30 + 10 = 90 Feet
2. L2 = $\sqrt{30^2 + 40^2}$ = $\sqrt{2500}$ = 50 feet
3. L1 - L2 = 90 - 50 = 40 Feet
4. Ella's walk to the oak tree was 40 feet farther than her walk back

FIGURE 5.6 Student's Completed Math Notes Organizer

How to Use the Strategy

A Math Notes organizer has five distinct sections labeled "The Facts," "The Questions," "The Steps," "The Diagram," and "The Solution." Often, a Math Notes organizer will also include helpful, thought-provoking sub-questions (as shown in Figure 5.6).

While the organizer provides a clear structure, many students still struggle with the actual problem-solving process. That's why we couple the Math Notes organizer with a simple but effective acronym known as SOLVER. SOLVER not only reminds students of the characteristic problem-solving elements but also of the sequence in which those elements can generally be completed. An enlarged version of SOLVER makes an excellent poster in almost any mathematics classroom (see Figure 5.7).

SOLVER

Set up the problem by listing the facts and determining what information is irrelevant and what information is missing from the problem.

Organize your thinking by asking, "What question needs to be answered?" and, "Are there any hidden questions that need to be answered?"

Look for ways to represent the problem either visually, physically, or both.

Verbalize your thinking by listing a plan, in words, of the steps you will take to solve the problem.

Execute the steps and solve the problem.

Reflect on your solution and check your work by asking, "Is the mathematics done correctly? Does my solution answer the question asked? Does my answer make sense?"

FIGURE 5.7   SOLVER Poster

The Strategy in Action

Elizabeth Jansson has the SOLVER poster prominently displayed in her eighth-grade algebra classroom. In the past few weeks, her students have been using the Math Notes organizer and SOLVER acronym with a variety of word problems. Today, she is introducing a new type of problem: distance-rate-time.

Elizabeth asks her students to take out a blank sheet of paper and draw the Math Notes organizer. Then, she presents this word problem:

> A cross-country bus is traveling away from San Francisco toward New York. At 9:15 AM, the bus has traveled ten miles towards its destination. At that time, a sports car leaves San Francisco on the same road, traveling in the same direction as the bus. The bus travels at 55 mph, while the car averages 70 mph. At what time would you expect the car to catch up to the bus?

Elizabeth then encourages her students to review and apply the SOLVER process as she moves around the room to observe students at work.

Set up the problem. In reading the problem, many students drew circles or boxes around each fact they found, while all students rewrote them in the Facts section of their Math Notes organizer (see the Facts box in Figure 5.8).

Organize your thinking. Students reread the problem, underline the key question to be answered, and transfer that question to the organizer. Elizabeth reminds students to think about important "hidden questions" that will need answering to solve the key question and write those down too (see the Questions box in Figure 5.8).

Look for ways to represent the problem visually. Verbalize your thinking. Students sketch a representation of the problem and develop a plan for solving it by listing the problem-solving steps (see the Diagram and the Steps boxes in Figure 5.8).

The Facts

What are the facts?

San Francisco is the initial starting point for both the bus and the car.

At 9:15 AM, the bus has gone 10 miles, and the car begins.

The bus's rate of speed is 55 mph, and the car's rate of speed is 70 mph.

What is missing?

The time both vehicles travel is missing.

What is irrelevant?

The car is a sports car.

New York is the destination for the bus.

The Steps

What are the steps needed to solve the problem?

1. Pick a variable for the car's driving time (t).
2. Write expressions for the distance traveled by the bus and the car after 9:15 AM.
3. Write an equation.
4. Solve the equation for time (t).
5. Answer the question by adding the driving time to the start time of 9:15 AM.

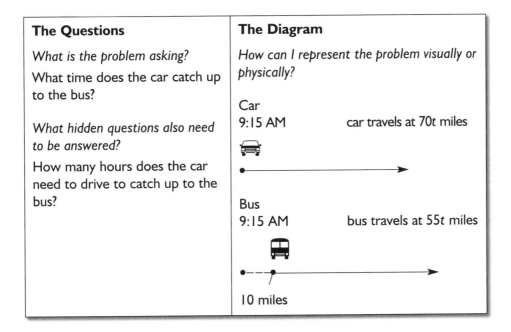

The Questions	The Diagram
What is the problem asking? What time does the car catch up to the bus? *What hidden questions also need to be answered?* How many hours does the car need to drive to catch up to the bus?	*How can I represent the problem visually or physically?* Car 9:15 AM car travels at 70*t* miles Bus 9:15 AM bus travels at 55*t* miles 10 miles

FIGURE 5.8 Math Notes Organizer for Car/Bus Problem

As students work, Elizabeth encourages them to meet with a learning partner to compare their Diagrams and Steps, to note similarities and differences, and to develop a final set of steps they both agree on. Meanwhile, Elizabeth moves around the classroom and takes time to applaud students' representations and to help them think through any glitches in their steps.

Now that students have worked through the "SOLV" of SOLVER, Elizabeth tells the class that they have completed the critical portions of the problem-solving process. She also reminds them that later in the unit, when they use this process to solve problems that will be graded, 50% of the credit will be based on their work in the four S, O, L, and V cells of the Math Notes organizer.

> *Execute the steps and solve the problem.* Students apply the problem-solving plan they developed in the Steps box to the problem, as shown in Figure 5.9.

The Solution

Let *t* = the time that the car drives after 9:15 AM

The car will then travel 70*t* miles and the bus 55*t* miles

$70t = 10 + 55t$

$t = \frac{2}{3}$ of an hour (or 40 minutes)

At 9:55 AM, the car should catch up to the bus.

FIGURE 5.9 The Solution (Using the Math Notes Organizer)

Reflect on your solution. After allowing students to look over and share their solutions, Elizabeth works through the steps in solving the problem on the board. To conclude the lesson, Elizabeth asks students to create a new section in their math notebooks for distance-rate-time problems and to insert this problem as their first example. For homework, students solve two additional distance-rate-time problems—one in which they need to solve for distance and one in which they need to solve for rate. The following day, Elizabeth begins with a discussion in which students share their solutions, discuss how they used Math Notes to arrive at their solutions, and explore the differences between the three different problems.

Why the Strategy Works

Math Notes is a highly effective teaching and learning strategy because it deals squarely with the challenges of problem solving in three ways.

1. Math Notes emphasizes the process *of problem solving!* As students use the Math Notes organizer and SOLVER, they come to see problem solving as a manageable, step-by-step *process* rather than a mysterious or frustrating hit-or-miss experience.

Of course, mathematicians have long thought about and generally agreed upon what good problem-solving strategies look like. For example, a half century ago, Hungarian mathematician George Polya (1957) wrote *How to Solve It*, a classic book that details the time-honored sequence of problem-solving steps. More recently, Robert Sternberg (1999) restated problem-solving steps in terms of abilities and added problem "representation" as a distinct ability. Figure 5.10 displays these two similar problem-solving approaches side by side.

The Math Notes strategy proceduralizes the strong agreement between these problem-solving models, equipping today's problem solvers to attack even the most difficult problems with confidence.

Polya: Basic Problem-Solving Steps	Sternberg: Key Problem-Solving Abilities
1. Understand the problem. 2. Devise a plan. 3. Carry out the plan. 4. Look back—examine and check the solution.	1. Identify the problem. 2. Represent the problem either mentally or visually. 3. Formulate strategies for solving the problem. 4. Plan before problem solving. 5. Assess work and process.

FIGURE 5.10 Polya's Steps and Sternberg's Abilities for Solving Problems

2. Math Notes makes the problem-solving process visible! The Math Notes organizer enables the learner to see how the key problem-solving elements—collecting facts, asking questions, representing the problem, and planning out the steps—are all interrelated. What's more, the organizer focuses students on their own progress in solving the problem and on what they need to do next.

3. Math Notes fosters good problem-solving habits! Regular use of Math Notes helps students develop key habits, such as

- Reading and rereading problems carefully;
- Identifying and answering questions in need of answers;
- Sketching meaningful and helpful pictures;
- Planning before acting;
- Thinking both arithmetically and algebraically (e.g., using variables and equations);
- Asking themselves if their answers are reasonable; and
- Even (*gasp!*) enjoying problem solving and problem-solving success!

Planning Considerations

One of the best things about Math Notes is that it is simple to implement, allowing you to focus much of your attention on students' problem-solving skills. Once you have taught the SOLVER process, it is essentially all about the problems you select. Here are some general guidelines for planning and using Math Notes in your classroom:

- Select rich word problems.
- Model the Math Notes process—perhaps two or three times.
- Distribute the organizer template—once students have used Math Notes a few times, there will be no need to reproduce the organizer; students can, and should, create their own.
- Use Math Notes frequently—practice with different kinds of word problems, and incorporate use of the Math Notes process into your assessments.
- Archive student work—encourage students to keep their work and use it as a reference to help them with new problems they encounter. A portfolio of a student's best Math Notes work makes for a wonderful parent-night collection!

Variations and Extensions

Stepping Before Leaping—Math Notes and Information Deprivation

Seventh-grade teacher Marguerite Taylor uses Math Notes often and has been stressing with students how critical the planning step is to the problem-solving process. Earlier in the year, she discovered that many of her students either could not distinguish planning from solving or simply could not resist doing it all at once. The idea occurred to her to withhold some of the critical facts needed for solving until students had essentially completed the "SOLV" portions of SOLVER.

For example, during a unit on three-dimensional figures, volume, and surface area, Marguerite presents problems in two parts. In the first part, students have no numbers to work with, which focuses their efforts on planning rather than solving. For example:

Part 1

> Marguerite holds up a solid foam brick. She asks students to look at the brick and internalize its shape in their minds. Then, she poses a question, "We know volume is calculated in cubic units, and surface area is calculated in square units. So, if we ignore the different units, which is greater in value, the prism's total surface area or its volume? (Note: Students will need to measure the prism's dimensions, but only after the S, O, L, and V in SOLVER have been completed and students are ready to solve in E (see poster in Figure 5.9).

Initially, Marguerite's students struggled to know how to complete the Facts, the Steps, and the Diagram sections of their Math Notes organizers without having numbers. However, as they talked through the question as a class, they realized that variables could be used! The organizer in Figure 5.11 is the product of a wonderful class discussion. (Marguerite later acknowledged that her heart jumped for joy!)

The Facts

Rectangular prism

　Length: ℓ = ___

　Width: w = ___

　Height: h = ___

The Steps

1. Measure the ℓ, w, and h of the object.

2. Write Volume formula,
   $V = \ell wh$, and substitute variable values.

3. Write the TSA formula,
   TSA $= 2\ell w + 2\ell h + 2wh$, and substitute variable values.

Compare TSA to V to determine which is greater.

The Questions

Which is greater in value, the rectangular solid's TSA or its V?

What is the V of the rectangular prism?

What is the TSA?

The Diagram

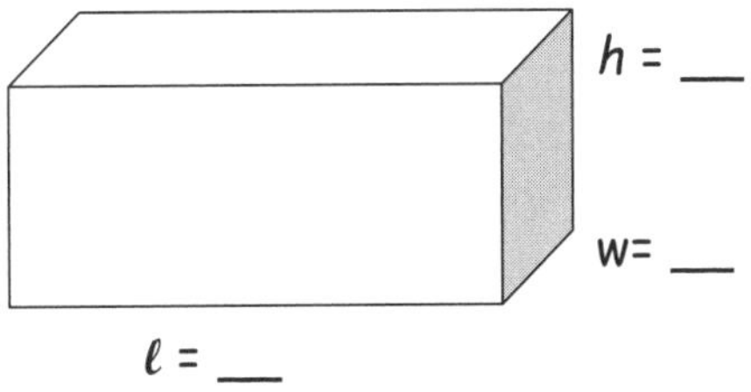

h = ___

w = ___

ℓ = ___

FIGURE 5.11 Partially Completed Math Notes (Without the Solution)

Part 2

Students measure the foam brick to determine its length, width, and height. Now, with such a solid understanding of the question and a set of clear steps for solving the problem, students input the numbers and complete their calculations.

$\{h = 2.5$ inches, $\ell = 9$ inches, and $w = 3$ inches$\}$

Students wrote the values in the blanks left in the Facts and the Diagram sections of their organizers and then easily followed their planned steps and completed the Solution section (Figure 5.12).

The Solution

1. $\ell = 9$ in. $w = 3$ in. $h = 2.5$ in.

2. $V = \ell wh = (9)(3)(2.5) = 67.5$ in^3.

3. $TSA = 2\ell w + 2\ell h + 2wh = 2(9)(3) + 2(9)(2.5) + 2(3)(2.5) = 114$ in^2.

4. The total surface area value (117) of this rectangular prism is greater than the value of its volume (67.5).

FIGURE 5.12   The Solution

After students have solved the problem, they take some time to reflect on the following question in their mathematics journals: In this problem, how were the variables essential to your planning? How does planning before solving help you build good problem-solving skills?

Organizer F: Math Notes Organizer

The Facts	**The Steps**
What are the facts?	What steps can we take to solve the problem?
What is missing?	
The Questions	**The Diagram**
What questions need to be answered?	How can we represent the problem visually?
Are there any hidden questions that need to be answered?	

The Solution

Integrated Math Engagement

Strategy Overview

Imagine that you could visualize and represent your students' understanding of mathematics. Now imagine that the typical student's understanding of mathematics looked like this:

_____

What would that line segment say about a student's understanding? Now, imagine that another student's understanding of mathematics looked like Figure 5.13:

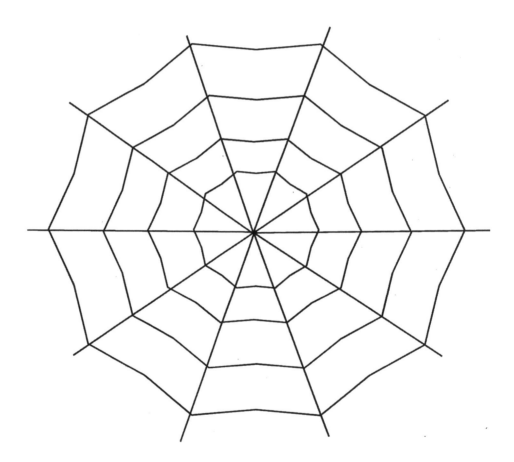

FIGURE 5.13 Spider Web

What would the spider web reveal about the student's understanding? What's the difference between understanding that looks like a line segment and understanding that looks like a spider web?

The difference can be summed up in a word: _connections._ If students spend their days in math class practicing isolated skills and memorizing text definitions and formulas, understanding may progress but it will remain flat and one-dimensional, like a line. If, on the other hand, students are engaged in interesting problem-solving activities that integrate multiple and related math concepts and skills, their minds will begin "shooting threads" as they discover the deeper connections that make mathematics so powerful and unique among disciplines.

Integrated Math Engagement is a strategy that encourages students to take an active role in discovering these connections. For example, all students learn about fractions, decimals, percentages, ratios, proportions, and probability. But, it is all too rare for students to explore how these concepts are interrelated. As a result, opportunities for students to draw on their prior knowledge, tease out patterns, and discover principles that unify the study of mathematics are missed. The line prevails over the spider web.

Integrated Math Engagement addresses this common problem head on. The strength of any Integrated Math Engagement lesson is tied directly to the design of the problems that students solve. Well-designed problems integrate a variety of interrelated concepts and skills and help students discover the hidden links between them.

How to Use the Strategy

Two things drive an Integrated Mathematical Engagement lesson: a set of related math concepts that follow a logical progression and a series of questions or tasks that lead students through the progression while highlighting important connections. We'll cover these in the "Planning Considerations" section. Assuming you have designed your tasks, here's how Integrated Math Engagement plays out in the classroom:

1. Introduce the activities or problems to be solved to the students. Explain their roles and your role during the lesson.

2. Review the key vocabulary and concepts students will need to understand and use during the lesson.

3. Model any skills or procedures students will need to apply.

4. Provide the materials students will need to work through the lesson.

5. Instruct students to work on the problems or challenges embedded in the lesson. Observe students while they work; provide feedback and coaching as needed. Work may be done individually, in groups, or both at different points in the lesson.

6. Encourage students to look for and explore interesting connections they find as they work.

7. Allow students to draw preliminary conclusions.

8. Use discussion time to help students articulate connections, refine their conclusions, and tie their learning back to the key terms and concepts identified at the outset.

The Strategy in Action

Carlo Valverde has delivered a series of isolated lessons in geometry and now wants his students to make deeper connections and pull these separate lessons together to form a more unified whole. Over the course of the previous lessons, Carlo and his students have addressed the following vocabulary, concepts, and skills.

Key Vocabulary:

polygon, regular polygon, hexagon, circle, inscribed, line segment, end points, consecutive vertices, nonconsecutive vertices, chord, radius, diameter, circle segment, area, ratio, congruence, similarity

Key Concepts and Understanding:

- The vertices of a regular polygon are evenly distributed or spaced on a circle in which the polygon is inscribed;
- The radii of any regular polygon divide the polygon into congruent equilateral triangles;
- Ratios of corresponding sides, perimeters, and areas resulting from similar figures; and
- Connections between addition, subtraction, multiplication, division, and areas of component regions of plane figures.

Skills:

- How to find measures of interior angles of a regular polygon
- How to find angle bisectors and midpoints of line segments
- How to find perimeter and area of plane figures, including triangle, hexagon, and circle

Carlo begins his Integrated Math Engagement by listing the key vocabulary terms on the board and reviewing their meanings with students. Once Carlo is comfortable with students' understanding of the key terms, he issues a challenge: He invites five students to the board to see who can draw the best regular hexagon by hand. Students rate each hand-drawn hexagon on a scale of 1 to 10, with 10 representing a perfect hexagon.

"Today," Carlo tells students, "I'm going to show everyone how to draw a hexagon that's a perfect 10. And best of all, once we've all drawn our perfect hexagons, we'll be able to make all kinds of important connections that we probably couldn't see before."

Carlo provides each student with a 360° circle protractor, plain white paper, a centimeter ruler, and two colored pencils. Using a transparency and overhead projector, Carlo then leads the students through the steps to create a "perfect 10" hexagon:

1. Place your protractor on your paper, so the zero degree mark is positioned as the number 3 would be on a clock. Then, using the protractor, trace a circle and mark its center.

2. Draw points at the 0, 60, 120, 180, 240, and 300 degree positions on the circle. Sixty degree intervals are used because 360 ÷ 6 vertices equals 60 degrees. Label these points A, B, C, D, E, and F. These points will be the vertices of the hexagon. Label the center of the circle and hexagon O.

3. Remove the protractor, and use the ruler to draw line segments that connect the six pairs of consecutive vertices. These line segments are the sides of the hexagon.

4. Draw six radii of the hexagon. These radii divide the hexagon into six congruent equilateral triangles.

5. Select one equilateral triangle, and draw its altitude.

6. Shade the six circle segments that form the region between the hexagon and the circle.

7. From the center of the hexagon, measure half way along each radius and mark the midpoint of each radius. Draw line segments that connect the six pairs of consecutive midpoints. This will form a hexagon that is smaller and similar to the original hexagon. Label these points R, S, T, U, V, and W (see Figure 5.14).

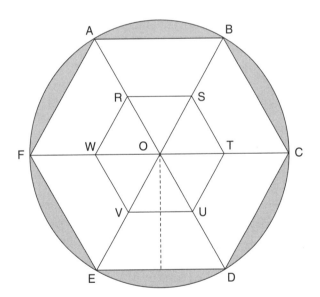

FIGURE 5.14 Two Perfect Hexagons

"OK," says Carlo. "Now that we've drawn two perfect hexagons, we're ready to begin exploring what we've got on our hands and see what kinds of connections we can make. Here's how we'll start."

Carlo has his students measure (to the nearest tenth of a centimeter) and label the following parts of the figure:

- Radius OF and diameter FC of the circle;
- Base ED of the equilateral triangle EOD; and
- Base VU of equilateral triangle VOU.

"What do you notice?" Carlo asks once students have completed their measurements.

Students determine that the measures of base ED and base VU are also measures of a side of the larger hexagon and side of the smaller hexagon, respectively.

Next, Carlo challenges students to use what they've learned so far to calculate

- Area of circle O;
- Area of triangle EOD;
- Area of triangle VOU;
- Perimeter of hexagon ABCDEF; and
- Perimeter of hexagon RSTUVW.

Carlo moves around the room while students work and helps students who are having difficulty. After all students have made their calculations, Carlo says, "Believe it or not, we're only at the tip of the iceberg in terms of what we can figure out using our hexagons."

Carlo tells his students that for the next challenge, he wants them to see if they can figure out

- The areas of both hexagons (six times the area of the respective component triangles);
- The area of the six circle segments (the area of the larger hexagon subtracted from the area of the circles);
- The area of one circle segment;
- The ratio of the perimeter of the smaller hexagon to the perimeter of the larger hexagon; and
- The ratio of the area of the smaller hexagon to the area of the larger hexagon.

For this portion of the lesson, Carlo allows students to work in small problem-solving groups. Problem-solving groups work together to make the calculations Carlo has assigned them. Carlo also encourages groups to see if they can discover any patterns that emerge. He invites students to make and test conjectures and draw some conclusions regarding the ratios of corresponding sides, radii, perimeters, and areas of the two hexagons. Each problem-solving group must agree on at least three conclusions that can be drawn based on the figure.

Carlo follows up with a discussion. He asks the groups to share their conclusions and to explain to the class how they came to their conclusions. As students share and discuss their findings, Carlo refocuses their attention on the key words on the board and asks students to make sure they're using these words as they communicate their findings. Carlo also records student conclusions on the board. If there is disagreement about any conclusions or if the conclusions are misconceived, Carlo works with the class to refine their conclusions to make sure they are mathematically sound.

Carlo ends the lesson with a return to the critical vocabulary. He provides a vocabulary term to a student and asks the student how it applies to the lesson they've just completed. Carlo reviews all the key terms in this way, until every word has been defined and linked directly to the content of the lesson.

Why the Strategy Works

Across the country, too many math curricula are *a mile long and only an inch deep*. As a result, many teachers present mathematics as a series of multiple isolated topics and lessons that rarely demonstrate important connections and the power associated with those connections. The Integrated Math Engagement strategy is designed to engage students in problem-solving activities that permit students to see and experience the deep connections between the vocabulary they're learning, the concepts they're developing, and the skills they're mastering. The strategy is especially powerful in the development of students' mathematical reasoning for five reasons:

1. *The strategy begins with teacher modeling and/or direct instruction.* In the early phases of an Integrated Mathematical Engagement, the teacher takes time to prepare students for the more analytical, problem-based phases that will come later. Vocabulary gets reviewed, skills get modeled, and procedures are taught directly.

2. *Students assume greater responsibility for their learning—gradually.* As the lesson progresses, the teacher's role diminishes, and students are encouraged and challenged to assume greater responsibility for what they're learning.

3. *The strategy offers multiple opportunities for formative assessment.* While it's true that the teacher's role diminishes, the teacher does not simply sit back and disappear. As students work through the various challenges and problems embedded in the lesson, the teacher observes the students working. Any sources of difficulty can be identified and corrected via coaching in real time.

4. *The strategy taps into the power of cooperative learning.* Often, the challenges and activities within an Integrated Math Engagement lesson lend themselves perfectly to cooperative learning. Allowing students to tackle difficult challenges together and bounce their ideas off each other increases their confidence and leads to better problem solving (not to mention improved social skills).

5. *The strategy helps students see the big picture of mathematics.* Integrated Math Engagement starts with specifics: key vocabulary, important concepts, and critical skills. What happens over the course of a lesson is that students develop a working model of how the specifics fit together. By the strategy's end, students are able to draw conclusions and articulate mathematically sound principles that reveal generalized understanding of the different pieces they've been working with.

Planning Considerations

In designing an Integrated Math Engagement activity, keep the following tips in mind:

1. Start small and finish big. Integrated Math Engagement activities work best when they begin with the basic elements of mathematics and progress in incremental steps toward higher levels of mathematics. This allows students to experience success early in the activity and move gradually into the more challenging stages of the activity. So, begin by selecting a set of math concepts or skills that connect and follow a natural progression of mathematical development. Logical progressions include

- Math facts, mental-math digit-product challenges, evaluating algebraic expressions with whole numbers, solving equations, and functions;
- Operations on fractions, complex fractions, algebraic expressions, equations, ratios and proportions, and probability;
- Function diagrams, set notation, inverse, function notation, graphing and plotting points, equations with two variables, systems of equations, and points of intersection; and
- Geometric shapes, algebraic representations, lines of symmetry, perimeter, area, transformations, three-dimensional shapes, surface area, and volume.

2. Get all the key information out on the table. Look closely at the individual elements in your progression. These are your core concepts. For each core concept, identify the key information students need to know and understand about each core concept. Use a simple organizer like the one in Figure 5.15 to extract the subconcepts, key vocabulary, and skills and procedures that are embedded in the core concept.

Core Concepts (Elements in the Progression)	Subconcepts	Key Vocabulary	Key Skills/Procedures

FIGURE 5.15 Extracting the Essentials

3. Get clear on the connections you want students to find. Now that you have your concepts, subconcepts, vocabulary, and skills spelled out, it's time to connect the dots. What connections do you want students to discover? For example, do you want students to develop a big-picture understanding of part-to-whole relationships by exploring the relationships between fractions, decimals, percentages, ratios, proportions, and probability? If so, what specific connections will students be focusing their attention on? Identify at least three specific connections you expect students to uncover during the lesson. If you can't identify at least three connections, that's usually a sign that the progression you have chosen is not a good candidate for an Integrated Math Engagement lesson.

4. Design your tasks and activities. What kinds of tasks and activities will best highlight the core concepts with the lesson and the connections you expect students to discover? What will the sequence look like?

5. Don't forget a management plan. Integrated Math Engagement requires you to create a thorough management plan. You will need to ask and answer these questions:

- How long will the sequence take to complete?
- How will the vocabulary, concepts, and skills be reviewed?
- What will your role be after the review?
- Will there be minilessons, modeling sessions, or direct instruction built into the sequence?
- What will students' roles be?
- What materials will students need?
- How will you release responsibility to students over the course of the lesson?
- Will students work individually, in groups, or both?
- How much time will you allow for discussion and reflection?
- How will you collect formative-assessment data over the course of the lesson?
- Will students have the opportunity to correct their work?
- Will you need to make any accommodations for students who are having difficulty?

Variations and Extensions

Almost any Integrated Math Engagement lesson can be extended to meet a variety of purposes. For example, for the hexagon activity discussed in "The Strategy in Action" section:

1. Students could be challenged to compute the areas of the hexagon by finding the areas of the component trapezoids that form each of the hexagons. Note that one diameter of a hexagon divides the hexagon into two congruent trapezoids.

2. Students could be challenged to draw a different regular polygon and repeat the steps of the activity. For example, a student might choose to draw a pentagon. The student would divide 360 degrees by 5 and determine that the vertices would be distributed around the circle in increments of 72 degrees. The radii of the pentagon would divide the pentagon into five congruent triangles.

3. With any Integrated Math Engagement lesson, students' work and final results can be compiled in a Microsoft PowerPoint slideshow or other media format and shared with other students or classes.

Another option for Integrated Math Engagement is to design a theme-based lesson. Rich Integrated Math Engagement lessons can be built around real-world themes, such as sports, architectural and graphic design, consumer affairs, and so on. For example, Sylvia Kurland developed an Integrated Math Engagement lesson around the theme of baseball. Her progressive problem set incorporated

- *Number sense and statistics.* Understanding and calculating baseball statistics including batting average, on-base percentage and earned-run average; Sylvia generates baseball-themed problems that sound like this:

> The second baseman's two-game performance can be summarized by combining the fractions (2 hits out of 3 at-bats) and (3 hits out of 5 at-bats). The result is the fraction (5 hits out of 8 at-bats). But note, the denominator 8 is not the common denominator between 3 and 5, the denominators of the original fractions. Explain how this can be mathematically sound.

- *Algebra.* Here's a sample problem involving standings:

> Together, the first- and last-place teams in the division have won 45 games. The last-place team won 5 less than half the number of games the first-place team won. How many games have the first- and last-place teams won?

- *Geometry.* Identifying and exploring the geometric shapes that are part of the game.
- *Probability.* Here is a sample problem using home runs:

> At a given point in the season, the first baseman has hit 20 home runs in 180 at-bats. Use this data to write a ratio, in fraction form, of home runs to at-bats. Using a percent, what is the probability that the first baseman might hit a home run on his next at-bat?

- *Data Analysis.* Sylvia used statistics and numerical standings to develop data-analysis problems like this one:

> In the division standings, the second-place team is 2.5 games behind the first-place team. What does this mean? Create a scenario where both teams become tied for first place. Explain your reasoning.

References

Adams, T. L. (2003). Reading mathematics: More than words can say. *Reading Teacher, 56*(8), 786–795. Bangert-Drowns, R. L., Kulik, J. A., & Kulik, C. C. (1991). Effects of classroom testing. *Journal of Educational Research, 85*(2), 89–99.

Alter, P., Satenstein, F. (Directors), Goodson, M., & Todman, B. (Producers). (1950, February 2–1967, September 3). *What's My Line?* [Television series]. New York: Columbia Broadcasting System (CBS).

Bruner, J. (1960). *The process of education.* Cambridge, MA: Harvard University Press.

Bruner, J. (1973). *Beyond the information given: Studies in the psychology of knowing.* Oxford, UK: W. W. Norton.

Butler, F. M. (1999). Reading partners: Students can help each other learn to read! *Education and Treatment of Children, 22*(4), 415–426.

Carter, T., & Dean, E. (2006). Mathematics intervention for grades 5–11: Teaching mathematics, reading, or both? *Reading Psychology, 27,* 127–146.

Chen, Z. (1999). Schema induction in children's analogical problem solving. *Journal of Educational Psychology, 91*(4), 703–715.

Cole, J. C., & McLeod, J. S. (1999). Children's writing ability: The impact of the pictorial stimulus. *Psychology in the Schools, 36*(4), 359–370.

Costa, A. R., & Kallick, B. (Ed.). (2000). *Discovering & exploring habits of mind.* Alexandria, VA: Association for Supervision and Curriculum Development.

Crismore, A. (Ed.). (1985). *Landscapes: A state-of-the-art assessment of reading comprehension research: 1974–1984. Final report.* Washington, DC: United States Department of Education. (ED 261 350).

DeVries, D. L., Edwards, K. J., & Slavin, R. E. (1978). Biracial learning teams and race relations in the classroom: Four field experiments using teams-games-tournaments. *Journal of Educational Psychology, 70*(3), 356–362.

Draper, R. J. (2002). School mathematics reform, constructivism, and literacy: A case for literacy instruction in the reform-oriented math classroom. *Journal of Adolescent & Adult Literacy, 45,* 520–529.

Erwin, J. C. (2004). *The classroom of choice: Giving students what they need and getting what you want.* Alexandria, VA: Association for Supervision and Curriculum Development.

Falacci, N., Heuton, C. (Creators), Scott, R., & Scott, T. (Producers). (2005–present). *Numb3rs* [Television series]. Los Angeles: The Barry Schindel Company & CBS.

Flores, M. M., & Kaylor, M. (2007). The effects of a direct instruction program on the fraction performance of middle school students at-risk for failure in mathematics. *Journal of Instructional Psychology, 34*(2), 84–94.

Fuchs, D., Fuchs, L. S., Mathes, P. G., & Simmons, D. C. (1997). Peer-assisted learning strategies: Making classrooms more responsive to academic diversity. *American Education Research Journal, 34*(1), 174–206.

Gardner, H. (1983). *Frames of mind: The theory of multiple intelligences.* New York: Basic Books.

Gardner, H. (1999). *Intelligence reframed: Multiple intelligences for the 21st century.* New York: Basic Books.

Gardner, H. (2006). *Multiple intelligences: New horizons in theory and practice.* New York: Basic Books.

Gobet, F., Lane, P. C. R., Croker, S., Cheng, P. C. H., Jones, G., Oliver, I., & Pine, J. M. (2001). Chunking mechanisms in human learning. *Trends in Cognitive Sciences, 5,* 236–243.

Good, T. L., & Brophy, J. E. (2003). *Looking in classrooms* (9th ed.). Boston: Allyn & Bacon.

Gregory, G. (2005). *Differentiating instruction with style.* Thousand Oaks, CA: Corwin.

Hall, R., Kibler, D., Wenger, E., & Truxaw, C. (1989). Exploring the episodic structure of algebra story problem solving. *Cognition and Instruction, 6,* 223–283.

Hashey, J. M., & Connors, D. J. (2003). Learn from our journey: Reciprocal teaching and action research. *The Reading Teacher, 57*(3), 224–232.

Hattie, J., Biggs, J., & Purdie, N. (1996). Effects of learning skills interventions on student learning: A meta-analysis. *Review of Educational Research, 66*(2), 99–136.

Hyerle, D. (2000). *A field guide to using visual tools.* Alexandria, VA: Association for Supervision and Curriculum Development.

Jenkins, J. R., Stein, M. L., & Wysocki, K. (1984). Learning vocabulary through reading. *American Educational Research Journal, 21*(4), 767–787.

Jensen, E. (2005). *Teaching with the brain in mind* (2nd ed.). Alexandria, VA: Association for Supervision and Curriculum Development.

Johnson, D. W., & Johnson, R. T. (1999). *Learning together and alone: Cooperative, competitive, and individualistic learning* (5th ed.). Boston: Allyn & Bacon.

Jung, C. (1923). *Psychological types* (H. G. Baynes, Trans.). New York: Harcourt Brace.

King-Sears, M. E., & Bradley, D. F. (1995). Classwide peer tutoring: Heterogeneous instruction in general education classrooms. *Preventing School Failure, 40*(1), 29–35.

Koedinger, K. R., & Tabachneck, H. J. M. (1994, April). *Two strategies are better than one: Multiple strategies used in word problem solving.* Paper presented at the annual meeting of the American Educational Research Association, New Orleans, LA.

Kroesbergen, E. H., & Johannes, V. L. E. H. (2003). Mathematics interventions for children with special educational needs. *Remedial and Special Education, 24*(2), 97–114.

Linn, M. C., & Eylon, B. (2006). Science education: Integrating views of learning and instruction. In P. Alexander & P. Winne (Eds.), *Handbook of educational psychology* (2nd ed., pp. 511–544). Mahwah, NJ: Lawrence Erlbaum Associates.

Ma, X., & Kishor, N. (1997). Assessing the relationship between attitude toward mathematics and achievement in mathematics: A meta-analysis. *Journal for Research in Mathematics Education, 28,* 26–47.

Mamchur, C. (1996). *A teacher's guide to cognitive type theory and learning style.* Alexandria, VA: Association for Supervision and Curriculum Development.

Marzano, R. J. (2004) *Building background knowledge for academic achievement: Research for what works in schools.* Alexandria, VA: Association for Supervision and Curriculum Development.

Marzano, R. J. (2006). *Classroom assessment & grading that work.* Alexandria, VA: Association for Supervision and Curriculum Development.

Marzano, R. J. (2007). *The art and science of teaching: A comprehensive framework for effective instruction.* Alexandria, VA: Association for Supervision and Curriculum Development.

Marzano, R. J., Pickering, D., & Pollock, J. (2001). *Classroom instruction that works: Research-based strategies for increasing student achievement.* Alexandria, VA: Association for Supervision and Curriculum Development.

McCarthy, B. (1982). *The 4mat system.* Arlington Heights, IL: Excel.

McClelland, D. C. (1994). The knowledge-testing educational complex strikes back. *American Psychologist, 49,* 66–69.

McKellar, D. (2008). *Math doesn't suck: How to survive middle school math without losing your mind or breaking a nail.* New York: Plume/Penguin Group.

Mosston, M. (1972). *Teaching: From command to discovery.* Belmont, CA: Wadsworth.

Myers, I. B. (1962/1998). *The Myers-Briggs type indicator.* Palo Alto, CA: Consulting Psychologists.

National Council of Teachers of Mathematics. (1989). *Curriculum and evaluation standards for school mathematics.* Reston, VA: National Council of Teachers of Mathematics.

National Council of Teachers of Mathematics. (2000). *Principles and standards for school mathematics.* Reston, VA: National Council of Teachers of Mathematics.

Paivio, A. (1990). *Mental representations: A dual coding approach.* New York: Oxford University Press.

Pajak, E. (2003). *Honoring diverse teaching styles: A guide for supervisors.* Alexandria, VA: Association for Supervision and Curriculum Development.

Polya, G. (1957). *How to solve it.* Princeton, NJ: Princeton University Press.

Pressley, M. (2006). *Reading instruction that works: The case for balanced teaching* (3rd ed.). New York: The Guilford Press.

Raphael, T. E., & Kirschner, B. M. (1985, April). *The effects of instruction in compare/contrast text structure on sixth grade students' reading comprehension and writing production.* Paper presented at the annual meeting of the American Educational Research Association, Chicago.

Rees, P. (Creator/Director), Lentle, T., Dallow, A., Farrell, A. (Directors), & Plavnik, J. (Executive Producer). (2003–present). *MythBusters* [Television series]. Dublin, Ireland: Beyond Production & Silver Spring, MD: Discovery Communications (Discovery Channel).

Scarpello, G. (2007). Helping students get past math anxiety. *Techniques, 82*(6), 34–35.

Silver, H. F., Brunsting, J. R., & Walsh, T. (2008). *Math tools, grades 3–12: 64 ways to differentiate instruction and increase student engagement.* Thousand Oaks, CA: Corwin.

Silver, H. F. & Perini, M. J. (2009). The eight Cs of engagement: How learning styles and instructional design increase student commitment to learning. In R. J. Marzano (Ed.), *Developing expert teachers, leading edge anthology on instruction.* Bloomington, IN: Solution Tree.

Silver, H. F., Strong, R. W., & Perini, M. J. (2001). *Tools for promoting active, in-depth learning* (2nd ed.). Ho-Ho-Kus, NJ: Thoughtful Education Press.

Silver, H. F., Strong, R. W., & Perini, M. J. (2007). *The strategic teacher: Selecting the right research-based strategy for every lesson.* Alexandria, VA: Association for Supervision and Curriculum Development.

Silver, H. F., Thomas, E., & Perini, M. J. (2003). *Math learning style inventory.* Ho-Ho-Kus, NJ: Thoughtful Education Press.

Sternberg, R. J. (1999). The nature of mathematical reasoning. In L. V. Stiff & F. R. Curcio (Eds.), *Developing mathematical reasoning in grades K-12: 1999 yearbook,* 37–44. Reston, VA: National Council of Teachers of Mathematics.

Sternberg, R. J. (2006). Recognizing neglected strengths. *Educational Leadership, 64*(1), 30–35.

Taba, H. (1971). *Hilda Taba teaching strategies program.* Miami, FL: Institute for Staff Development.

Thomas, E. J. (2008). *Ask Dr. Math.* Fayetteville, GA: Dimension 2000.

Thomas, E. J. (2009a). *High achievement math program, grade 7.* Fayetteville, GA: Dimension 2000.

Thomas, E. J. (2009b). *High achievement math program, grade 8.* Fayetteville, GA: Dimension 2000.

Thomas, E. J., & Roe, T. (2009). *Transformation creation* [Computer software]. Fayetteville, GA: Dimension 2000.

Thoughtful Education Press. (2007). *Questioning styles and strategies: How to use questions to engage and motivate different styles of learners.* Ho-Ho-Kus, NJ: Author.

Thoughtful Education Press. (2009). *Math tools for three-dimensional figures* (curriculum guide). Ho-Ho-Kus, NJ: Author.

Whimbey, A., & Lochhead, J. (1999). *Problem solving and comprehension* (6th ed.). Mahwah, NJ: Lawrence Earlbaum Associates.

Wilkins, J. L. M., & Ma, X. (2003). Modeling change in student attitude toward and belief about mathematics. *Journal of Educational Research, 97*(1), 52–63.

Wormeli, R. (2005). *Summarization in any subject: 50 techniques to improve student learning.* Alexandria, VA: Association for Supervision and Curriculum Development.

Zbiek, R. M., Heid, M. K., Blume, G. W., & Dick, T. P. (2007). Research on technology in mathematics education: A perspective of constructs. *Second Handbook of Research on Mathematics Teaching and Learning, 2,* 1169–1207.

Index

CORWIN

A SAGE Company

The Corwin logo—a raven striding across an open book—represents the union of courage and learning. Corwin is committed to improving education for all learners by publishing books and other professional development resources for those serving the field of PreK–12 education. By providing practical, hands-on materials, Corwin continues to carry out the promise of its motto: **"Helping Educators Do Their Work Better."**